Wide Open Spaces

of related interest

Low-Demand Parenting
Dropping Demands, Restoring Calm, and Finding
Connection with your Uniquely Wired Child
Amanda Diekman
ISBN 978 1 83997 768 8
eISBN 978 1 83997 769 5
Audiobook ISBN 978 1 39981 204 7

The Strengths-Based Guide to Supporting Autistic Children
A Positive Psychology Approach to Parenting
Claire O'Neill
ISBN 978 1 83997 215 7
eISBN 978 1 83997 216 4

Things I Got Wrong So You Don't Have To
48 Lessons to Banish Burnout and Avoid Anxiety for Those Who Put Others First
Pooky Knightsmith
ISBN 978 1 83997 267 6
eISBN 978 1 83997 268 3

Wide Open Spaces

A Wellbeing Journal for Parents
of Neurodiverse Children

LOUISE FEARN

Illustrated by Imogen Fearn and Wilf Fearn

Jessica Kingsley Publishers
London and Philadelphia

First published in Great Britain in 2025 by Jessica Kingsley Publishers
An imprint of John Murray Press

1

A CIP catalogue record for this title is available from the
British Library and the Library of Congress

ISBN 978 1 80501 301 3

Printed and bound in Great Britain by TJ Books Ltd

Jessica Kingsley Publishers' policy is to use papers that are natural,
renewable and recyclable products and made from wood grown in
sustainable forests. The logging and manufacturing processes are expected
to conform to the environmental regulations of the country of origin.

Jessica Kingsley Publishers
Carmelite House
50 Victoria Embankment
London EC4Y 0DZ

www.jkp.com

John Murray Press
Part of Hodder & Stoughton Ltd
An Hachette Company

The authorised representative in the EEA is Hachette Ireland,
8 Castlecourt Centre, Dublin 15, D15 XTP3, Ireland (email: info@hbgi.ie)

For Imogen, who made me a mother all those years ago, who has the courage to question me when I'm getting it wrong, and who lovingly forgave me when I didn't see, at first, all of who she was. I'm a better person for knowing and loving you.

For Wilf, who so generously allowed me to share our story. You have shown us all how to live life on our own terms and to not bend for others when it might break you. Thanks for showing me the door to that wide open space, buddy. You freed us, and for that I will be forever grateful.

And for Steve, my co-pilot, who sings loudly to the radio early in the morning, made me coffee on difficult days, was subjected to most of my ponderings and has always been right there beside me on this journey of parenthood.

I love you all, xxx

Contents

Preface

I'm not an expert in neurodiversity.

Nor can anyone be, in my opinion. Of all the neurodiverse people I've ever met, every one of them is an individual. Their needs, interests and triggers have occasionally over-lapped but have also been utterly different. And so, it makes sense to me that we should only ever expect to be an expert of our individual selves and to guide our children to be the expert of *themselves* through exploration.

In that aspect I *am* experienced and along the way I have established many coping strategies for keeping balanced amidst day-to-day life, in an often dysregulated family.

I am not nailing this. I am in the thick of it, with you. But from time to time when I can get my head above water, I manage to course-correct. I ask myself and my family a lot of questions, and I get curious about the answers; and each time things get a little clearer and a little better for everyone.

I've also read a ton of books, done some courses and listened to hours of podcasts on the subjects of neurodiversity, communication strategies, mental health and healing practices. Many of those resources were created by people who claimed to be on the other side, having solved their problems or from a professional, expert background. They often made me feel more inadequate and overwhelmed by the task.

But during my journey and often in unusual places that don't always directly relate to the ways of the brain or parenting, I have picked up some actually useful techniques, little gems, that I continually call upon.

I've shared these ideas with my friends and now I offer them, along with this journal, to you.

Introduction: The Thing

I feel obliged, as a parent just like you, to tell you right from the start, and before you invest any time in reading further, that this journal is not going to be *the thing*.

It's a bold statement, I know, an unattractive disclaimer, to say out loud that it's not going to be the thing that solves all your problems, that makes you a parenting genius or your time at home with your child smooth-running. Please give me a moment to explain.

What I mean is it's not going to be *that* thing, the one we all hope will pull everything else together, like the mentor we're hoping our child will find at school or out in the community: that cool and breezy adult that will just get them and be patient and an excellent role model (whilst preferably also casually guiding them through some low-level qualification or a Duke of Edinburgh's Award).

And yeah, it's not going to be that amazing keyworker or teaching assistant that supports them just like you would. And it's not going to be like them finding their passion-hobby – the one that they are genius at and decide to make a career out of later in life.

It's not going to be that course that makes you understand how everything works, the ideal medication or that sensory input or stimulation that means that all the other symptoms melt away and your child now knows how to regulate themselves.

It's not going to do any of those things.

How I've gripped tightly to the hope that the next thing will be the thing that soothes our souls, is the missing piece of the jigsaw puzzle, our saviour.

I'm sorry to say that for years I leaped from one hopeful thing to the next, always being disappointed, until my friend, an occupational therapist (who deals all day with parents of neurodiverse and anxious children) said, 'I'm often met with that same gleam of hope when parents arrive at their appointments, and I hate the feeling of that impossible expectation.'

'I guess it's a journey,' I said, feeling dismayed myself at hearing her words, but also seeing how impossible it was for her, or any professional, to solve all our issues. 'They're entering into an exploration and you're the facilitator. You don't need to have all the answers. You just need to have all the right questions.'

Some days we're full of fight and other days we're defeated, but more often than not, we arrive at these appointments hungry and with huge expectations. With desperation. Please be the thing that makes it all ok. After a while, we, the parents, enter these appointments rigid with tension, on the edge of tears if anyone shows any kindness... or numb and disassociated.

The truth (and you probably don't want to hear this, but it'll save you a lot of heartbreak) is that the only person that is coming to save you... is you.

It's us.

It's actually a liberating concept once you lean in it, I promise. You cannot change the way in which you or your child's brain is wired, and I'd hazard a guess that you actually wouldn't want to. There's so much richness and beauty in our individuality after all. But, as an overloaded parent, just think how different the whole picture would look if you could be in this family experience and be reconnected with your sense of self. If you could learn to soothe yourself, bring yourself back to life and start living creatively: not only would the whole family benefit, but the issues you're currently facing would no longer be at the centre of your life. They'd be part of life's tapestry.

You'd also be giving your children a roadmap for their own adult lives, showing them that mums and dads are more than their roles, that parents and carers are people too, who need to feel whole and meet their own needs in order to function well.

Despite how much they call for snacks and later bedtimes, and get fired up in response to emotions, no child wants the responsibility of a parent that is dead inside due to their overwhelm or burnout. How much we do the therapeutic work so that we can meet our needs and live a joyful experience is completely up to us and just as much our responsibility as caring for our children.

And if your children live so far into their behaviours and reactions that even in adult life they cannot have this level of reflection, that's ok. You will thank your past self for it, for protecting your sanity so that you could keep on supporting all those years.

If your child lacks empathy or understanding for you as an individual beyond what you can offer them in terms of love and comfort, you may need to learn to advocate for yourself as well as you do for them.

Of course, there are still times when I feel the hope of some new shiny person or thing that is dangled before me. But now I see that for what it is and have a laugh with my friends at my own expense.

There's no one coming.

It's me and it's you and it's all of us.

Hopefully, throughout this book you'll find a sense of shared peace. We'll be there to hold each other's hands and give each other a quick squeeze each time our day falls apart, and we'll look together in awe, on the good days, at what we've created.

I'll be there with all the questions. The ones that are going to help lead you back to yourself, show you how to stay balanced through all the difficult moments and then help you find your children beneath those behaviours. Each question is an invitation to get to the bottom of the situation, what's in your heart, your truth. You can answer them out loud or in this journal, but I recommend you write them down if you possibly can. Even if they end up being sparse or a bit scribbly. Journalling is more about the act. It's an act of self-care. And jotting things down can unlock the unconscious mind and reveal things you didn't know were there. It's also active, and this sort of forward motion can help you shift repetitive patterns in your life and move beyond any stuck places you might be experiencing right now. If you fill in this journal and begin to try out some of the ideas and see what works for you, you will start to become 'the thing' for yourself, just as I have, to connect more easily with your kids and to shape each day into a life that's fulfilling.

The secret to journal success: Don't allow yourself to skip along, wolfing down the info and telling yourself you'll come to the questions later, when you have a pen or are less tired. Only continue on when you have thought about and answered each of the questions. Then you will have gone through the exploration part of the book by the time you come to the end and be on your journey to discovering and centring yourself.

I'm here right with you (tired and penless), and so is every other parent reading this. We're all here together. Go grab that pen and let's begin.

You may want to consider identifying a journal buddy – another parent that can hold you accountable to filling it in. I am currently doing this. We meet once a week and read out our answers and encourage each other to dig deeper. Knowing our meetings are coming up reminds me to spend time reading and filling out the next few sections.

PART ONE

A healing balm for stress and overwhelm

The Gap

There are days when I feel like Mary Poppins, and I'm patient and curious and organized. I work around the lack of attention span, the constant requests for food and screens and lack of interest in all pre-prepared activities, and we still somehow glide through the day. But more often than not, I'm tired and it's all been A LOT, and I'm unbalanced myself, and my capacity to deal with the next thing that's a problem is lacking. In this state I'm far more likely to shout or swear or cast ridiculously useless threats about the room that involve me taking stuff away or not doing the helpful things I said I would.

It's easy for me to get to that place a million times a day when I'm being a referee to siblings, shouted at, poked, not listened to, constantly required to stop what I'm doing to support others and generally dealing with everyone's dysregulation. I become completely dysregulated myself. Throw in a cold, a sick pet or a work problem, and things spiral fast.

Years ago, I went on a course about how to deal with challenging behaviours in children. The main advice given all the way through was to 'put on your own oxygen mask first' before helping your child put on theirs. It's an image taken from the flight safety sheets on an airplane. The thinking behind it is if you're taking airless seconds to help your child, then you might not get to your own air supply in time, in which case you would then be useless to your child. Gruesome imagery but it does make sense.

It stayed with me long after the other elements of the course had faded away. I was always attending to everyone else's needs first and ignoring my own. Our culture, after all, praises parents (particularly women) for being selfless, and we're steered into becoming martyrish, feeling guilty or defensive if we allocate time to nurture ourselves, let alone have fun. Men can also fall victim to society's expectations, feeling strongly that they must provide everything for their family.

And our own childhood experiences too can affect our ability to voice and meet our own needs as an adult.

My capacity to be present and balance others goes up and

down throughout the day and the week, but I tend, like many parents, to just keep going because there's so much to be done. I also have a sense, in another part of my brain, that if I run myself into the ground, get stressed, depressed or sick, I'm not going to be a useful resource or point of comfort for my kids. And yet, crazily, I still do it.

When the kids were young, my husband and I sometimes argued over who was more tired. How does anyone decide who does the dinner or bedtime routine when you've both been working hard all day?

Dr Brené Brown, an American research professor, came up with a strategy called the family gap plan. She explains that there is this myth that lasting relationships are 50/50:

> Strong, lasting relationships happen when your partner, or friend or whoever you're in relationship with, can pony up that 80% when you are down to 20, and that your partner also knows that when things fall apart for him or her, and they only have 10% to give, you can show up with your 90, even if it's for a limited amount of time.

Interesting. If you had to put a percentage on what parenting capacity you're running on right now, what figure would you give out of 50 (or out of 100 if it's all on you)? ...I'd say I'm currently about a 35/50.

Recognizing where we are and putting a number on it is actually very helpful. It helps you notice that things can change very quickly throughout the day. Brené and her husband would have conversations that went like this:

> Brené: 'Look, I'm on the edge. I got a solid 15 right now.'
> Steve: 'I was at 15, I'm up to 40.'
> Brené: 'We got a gap. 15 plus 40, 55, we got a 45 gap.'

You may well have a gap, but when you know where everyone is, you also have a better understanding of the situation and are more able to stay united.

For Brené, her gap problem was based around both her and her husband having full-on jobs. When hers took her away on tour, Steve, her husband, was working full-time and sorting the house and kids. When she came back, both of them were at a low of 20% and arguments broke out about who was going to pick up the slack.

The general premiss is that after working and outside all the other parts of life that require our energy (appointments, ageing parents, household chores, pet care, etc.), we then have to split the parenting between whoever has the capacity.

The requirement to parent (where your child or children are at and what they need from you will fluctuate) can be at any moment 100% from the pair of you as a unit; and when you're feeling refreshed and ready to meet those needs, you can give 100% support and attention as required, divided between you.

Perhaps some days you do indeed have 50% and your partner can meet the other 50. Sometimes one of you will step up when the other is away, ill or stressed out.

We can give 80 or 90% in bursts for a limited time when we have capacity. For all the single parents reading this, yep that 100 falls onto you but can be offset by any help you get from grandparents or friends. It's a tough one.

And what if you are also neurodiverse? Or your partner? It's usually passed down genetically after all, or have some of those boxes ticked such as lacking organizational skills, getting easily frustrated or being less able to see things from other people's perspectives?

After a lot of fights, Brené and her husband asked the question: What do we do when we both only have 20% to give and the situation requires more? They formed a family gap plan for these moments.

Being a parent of neurodiverse children often feels like full capacity is met and exceeded very quickly. In our household I can tell you that who we all are means that limits are met without anyone going away!

When I heard about Brené's gap I was shocked.

It made me realize how different and challenging having a neurodiverse family is, because we're nearly always working from a consistent gap. I think a lot of single parents are too.

What if you're a single parent with neurodiverse children? Well, I see you and I see your gap. You're doing the absolute best you can.

Before the pandemic, both my husband and I were working from home but trying to complete as many hours as possible to get through project deadlines. My daughter, who has undiagnosed dyslexia and ADHD, was about to sit her GCSEs but had hit a wall. She was so stressed out by an education system that didn't fit her, that something inside her had snapped. She was refusing to revise, attend school or sit any exams. She'd never refused school. She was Head Girl. But she couldn't take another minute of it.

My son was also suffering. Having not coped in mainstream primary, he was in Year 7 at a small, independent school that was falling into special measures. The staff lacked SEN expertise and he was jumping the gate and running home most days. He was also feeling suicidal at times. We were trying to get a formal educational plan sorted out for him whilst funding the independent school fees through charitable donations and work done for the school on their website.

I think, looking back, I was close to some sort of mental breakdown. I'm not entirely sure what my percentage would have been back then, but under 10 I reckon. I was barely making each day. I could feel the stress in my body constantly. A pounding head, a racing heart, a tight knot in my chest. Everything made me cry. Then boom. We were in lockdown. No school. No exams. My project was put on hold.

I think the pandemic, after I got past the fear we were all going to die like plague victims, actually saved my mental health and that of my family.

It was an opportunity to see how all those things didn't add up to something that could be maintained. I was trying to tick all the boxes, but at the detriment of our mental health. The truth at the heart of it all was that school wasn't healthy for my children and I couldn't work full-time and support them in it. It wasn't viable, and something had been about to break.

Why on earth does a parent or child have to be at breaking point before we give ourselves permission to go against society's expectations and do what's right for us as a family?

I invite you to consider each member of your immediate family. Think about what they can and can't manage right now. How much time and energy do you as a parent have to support them when they need it? Between you and your partner is it enough? Does your day-to-day situation add up?

PAUSE AND REFLECT

Take a moment to write down how you balance earning money, supporting the children at school/college or at home and how you meet or don't meet your own needs. Is there a consistent and substantial gap or one that just crops up from time to time?

If it helps: set a timer for six minutes telling yourself you can stop thinking/writing when it is up. But feel free to carry on thinking and writing about it should you want to! Explore the situation as much as you can. And be brave in your thinking. It's hard to admit that school or a job isn't right or is too much, but it's important to make these truths visible, even if for now it's just to yourself. There will be an element of instinct to the answers. Feel about for it. Who is coping? How much do they require of you to cope? Overall is this sustainable or overwhelming?

Things to consider:

- What does everyone in your household do in their day/ free time/weekend?

- How capable are they doing it (physically and emotionally)? There are a lot of invisible factors. Think about whether you or they need waking up, motivating, organizing, lifts, lunch, homework support, mental health support.)

- Are you (and your partner if you have one) coping with your own load and the support required by your children?

- Is each of your children coping with their daily or weekly load? Do some things tip them or you over the edge? Do the activities all of you partake in add value to your self-esteem?

Brené said that when they identified that they were not 100% between them, then they moved into the gap plan with all seriousness. It involved everyone in the family identifying where they were at so that the whole family were on the same page. Then:

- Eight hours' sleep minimum.

- Movement, as our bodies store anxiety.

- Eating well (when you're tired, you're more likely to snack on sugary stuff and then crash and then snack again).

- No harsh words (kindness towards each other).

- No nice words with harsh faces (authentic kindness).

- Say you're sorry (and real apologies acknowledge the hurt you've caused someone else).

- Accept all apologies with 'thank you'.

- Light-hearted family time.

Now that's Brené's plan. That's what she, her husband and children sat down and came up with for them. All families are different. I know that some of the stuff on her list we have to do on the regular because we often live with a gap; and some would actually be very ambitious for us, during a big capacity gap, to execute. I think my own gap plan would look like this:

- Permission to clear the diary of anything non-essential.

- Movement and slow, deep breaths out – where possible a run or walk in nature if only for 10–20 minutes or something similar that completes the stress cycles (see Chapter 2).

- Soft clothes – pyjamas and loungewear if at home.

- Kindness to self and others (in the form of letting the little things go).

- A nutritious meal – I'd use my last bit of energy on that and really home in on what I felt like eating.

- Time to unwind before bed with stretches, some reflexology (self-care) and lavender spray.

- A good sleep.

That's what I alone would need to re-balance. To achieve this, I'd need to focus on the above list and let some of my parenting ideals go. Perhaps the kids would be watching TV and snacking on cereal whilst I got the meal together. Perhaps all day. Maybe I need stir-fried cabbage to feel sane and I just throw in some fishfingers for them if they didn't feel like eating stir-fry. Maybe I'd read for an hour and then hold the fort whilst my husband did something he likes. I'd lose my TV time to make sure I wound down properly and went to bed early. I might get up early to have an hour to myself to run, meditate or plan a meal I actually feel like eating.

Switching off the TV, going to bed early and getting up early feel like sacrifices to start with. They don't feel easy, but I always feel better for doing those things. Over time they have started to feel like a gift to my eight-hours-in-the-future self.

If the kids are also up to capacity during a family gap – say those times when everyone is ill or has stressful situations going on in their lives – then that's the moment to show them, model for them what true self-care looks like.

Knowing that when I give myself permission to be kind and loving towards myself and to take care of my needs I am role-modelling this for my husband and children; giving them permission to attend to their needs has been a very freeing concept for me. I think it's freed us all. When I take time to make sure I'm ok, this gives my husband permission to do the same. Suddenly we're encouraging each other to do those things rather than being resentful or competitive over free time. And we're showing our children a better relationship dynamic.

And do I want my daughter to become a martyr in her own role as a mother should she wish to have children? No, I don't. Or my son. If I wouldn't want it for them, then it's also not healthy for me. I live by that thought these days. Because I always want what's best for them and I don't always allow myself what's best for me.

I know, from experience, that it feels somehow wrong/ selfish/misguided to attend to your needs when everything is falling apart around you and you are up to your ears in problem situations, but actually, you'll soon see that in doing so, you're in a much brighter and more balanced place to support others. You'll have more capacity for everything. And it's pretty essential in the long run.

PAUSE AND REFLECT

What would putting on your oxygen mask first look like for you?

In other words what actions would you need to take during a gap in order to have more capacity to parent? This is your moment to figure out what your own family gap plan looks like.

I'd need to...

. . . .

. . . .

. . . .

. . . .

We'd need to...

. . . .

. . . .

. . . .

. . . .

When there was a consistent gap in our life something had to change. I had to give up work and we needed to live off a much smaller income with the help of some government benefits.

Eventually we would give up many things to survive. School with its packed lunches, doorstep refusals, school runs and homework. Then attempts at home education. For a while we just focused on staying mentally and emotionally balanced.

We gave up tidying the house along with nagging the children to tidy. With that, out went inviting people over (with the exception of very close friends or family who accepted the situation without judgement.) We gave up holidays abroad some years and holidays that were a step too far, such as camping. We couldn't consider hosting Christmas. Christmas cards went. Birthday shopping for other people outside of the family had to go, with apologies. We gave up making our children clean their teeth twice a day and eventually, as they got older, even screen time limitations.

On good days, when things felt more peaceful, we added something more in: a play date, a family surf trip or extra time off for the adults.

We didn't need to give up meeting our own needs. We needed, if anything, to meet them more. But we had to give up on some of society's expectations, including those of our friends and families.

- If you find that there is a consistent gap you probably need outside help. It may be you are entitled to state benefits that allow you to work less and have more time to care for your child. In the UK you can apply for the Disability Living Allowance. It is a tax-free benefit that does not consider your income. There are different pay levels depending on your child's need. They do not need to have an Education, Health and Care Plan (EHCP) for you to apply for this, but you may need a simple letter from your school or doctor.

- Some households can also get respite enablers. The NHS website for Children and Family Health can help you to request this.

- Perhaps a family member or friend can offer a morning or two a week to help you out. Grandparents/other parent friends/older siblings (where appropriate) often look after toddlers in and around their nursery sessions to help out tired or working mums. This is a similar situation. Ask around to find out who can spare a few hours or a morning.

- Where none of the above is available, read on! You're going to need to take radical care of yourself and I've got you covered.

Stress Responses

When you are regularly stressed throughout the day, it's useful to get into the practice of completing the stress cycle.

During a moment of stress, your body produces hormones such as adrenaline and cortisol. They flood the body and can stay there.

Adrenaline suppresses your appetite (did you know that it's the reason anxious children find it hard to eat breakfast before school or their lunch?), and it's also toxic. It exists to get you out of a tight spot, such as the often quoted caveman running from a sabre-toothed tiger, and didn't evolve with the expectation of being called upon daily.

The good news is there are a few things that can help your body flush out the adrenaline, calm the vagus nerve and nervous system and get you back on track. The vagus nerve (pronounced like Las Vegas but spelled differently) plays a role in a lot of critical functions, a couple of which are controlling your heart rate and regulating the stress response (fight, flight or freeze). Basically, the vagus nerve's job is to calm you down, and then keep you calm.

Here's a list of things that help the vagus nerve calm you down:

- Cold water splashed on your face (this could be a cool flannel).

- Certain reflexology and acupressure spots on the foot and face (around the ear) also calm the nervous system. There are lots of short YouTube videos that demonstrate these, and they are great for kids with ADHD or autistic brain types.

- Deep breaths out – my son and I use a guided breathwork practitioner called Taylor Somerville but there are many to choose from. It's free on the Insight Timer app. We always do this together.

- A shower can reset the energy (a cold one is even better!)

- Dancing – most of us can't get our teenagers to join in with this but a quick kitchen dance whilst you're getting tea ready might well help you out!

- Shaking it out.

- Crying and laughing.

- Singing – belt one out in the car or shower.

- Hugs; the hugger must be roughly the same height – so not leaning in to you or pulling you – and the hug must last for 20 seconds or more to do the job!

- Exercise.

- Nature, especially bare feet on the ground.

- Acts of creativity – painting, drawing, making music, writing, crafts, etc.

- Grounding/centring or embodiment meditations.

- Cold-water swimming.

- Drinking a glass of water.

- Flower remedies.

And no, I'm not for a minute suggesting that drinking a glass of water solves everything. That would be bonkers. Individually, none of the things on the list will make the situation go away. And that's where a lot of people trip up. They don't see the point. But the magic is in the process...

The time I take to identify my emotions when selecting flower remedies from a list helps me to name them. Running the tap for cold water, filling a glass and drinking it are an act of self-care that my body subtly notices. It also gives me precious seconds to reflect and observe. I drink the water or splash my face and I think ok, I've ticked a couple of easy things off. How am I now? What else could I add from the list above? Ten minutes of breathwork, a snack, a song or a run? Before I know it a combination of these things, and the time it takes to feel into what I need next, have got me back on track.

The real magic is first in the realization that you are stressed and need to help yourself before you go on, and then in the thought processes and small string of actions that follow.

I go through phases, but for me, right now, it's the breathwork. I walk around in my day blowing out long deep breaths that make my kids raise their eyebrows. I listen to freebie breathwork sessions on my phone. Six minutes of Grounding Breathwork in the supermarket carpark, three minutes Emergency Re-balance on the way to a pickup, eight minutes of Mid-Morning Stress Relief whilst my coffee cools, eleven minutes of Handling Stress in the Moment whilst in the shower.

When things get really bad, I go for a walk, meditate or drive 25 minutes to the sea and get in there. Yes, all year round, and it's cold in the UK. I don't wear a wetsuit as that spoils the effect on my brain, but I also don't manage more than a few minutes in winter. It's a desperate dash in and out but it does the job. It makes me yell and swear and laugh at myself and sing for some reason, to keep myself moving as I wade in. And there are always rivers if you don't live near the sea. Even swimming in a pool can be effective.

A friend of mine formed a local WhatsApp group. It started with a few other friends who were interested. They added their friends and now there is always a friend or a friend of a friend to buddy up with and meet at the beach carpark. The women I know swim at dawn for 20 minutes. It's meant to be great for the peri-menopause/menopause too, but as my son Wilf just pointed out when he read this, I'm more of a gingerly-edge-in, in-moments-of-crisis, shrieky type of wild swimmer. So, I don't go with the group.

For another friend of mine, reaching out by text in a difficult moment is a help. Her texts state that they require no reply or solutions. They are just her putting down some feelings and having them known and witnessed.

My family like reflexology points on our feet and head being pressed, especially if someone else is doing it! Guided breathwork, a cool shower and water on the face are also our emergency go-to's.

After the stress cycle (whether it is completed or not) everyone is tired out. Sometimes after a big upset (like a loss, a school exclusion or difficult medication trial) everyone is tired for days and we all need to cut ourselves some slack. And take the pressure off the whole household. This is 'the soft landing place'. It's a more laid back, smoother version of the family gap plan, which can roll on for weeks or as long as required!

PAUSE AND REFLECT

This week have a go at completing the stress cycle. List the ideas and stick them on the fridge if you need to and try to tick off three to five of them when stressed.

Out of the bigger practices (exercise, swimming, meditation, breathwork), what could you dust off or try out so that it's in your back pocket for those tricky moments?

I invite you to create an intention here. Write down one or two of the bigger things you will try out in the next few days before moving on with the journal.

I'll try out...

. . . .

. . . .

. . . .

. . . .

When?

....

....

....

....

How did you get on? And what might you try next?

....

....

....

....

....

....

....

....

The Soft Landing Place

The soft landing place can be seeing your best friend (or texting them), or it can be the week ahead if you take out all the commitments in the diary. It can be super-soft loungewear or your favourite hoodie with the cosy lining or a blanket on the sofa. It's foods that don't confront your child, balanced meals, plenty of drinks and a settling in to the comfort of the winding-down/bedtime routine with ease, time and patience. It's everyone staying in their comfort zones and has the same feel as a pyjama day on a relaxed holiday. It's baggy parenting with room for everyone to breathe, even if that means the children are on their screen a bit more. For kids with anxiety the screen is often a safe place for escape.

When stress occurs, this is the exact moment to execute a bit of self-care. Ok, a lot of self-care and self-compassion. Go hard on it. Talk to yourself the way you'd speak to your friend if they were in your situation. You'd say to them, 'Awww sweetheart, you do such a great job. It's not easy, is it? But I see you. You're a great mum/dad/bonus parent/carer, bless you, always fighting for them, giving them a voice. You really do your best. And that's all we can ever do. I mean, ffs/good grief/holy moly, make yourself a cup of tea and have a break. Rest for a moment.' If you find summoning up this level of kindness and compassion hard, if it sounds a little cringy to you, then this is an interesting little signal that you could benefit from attending to this area.

For parents navigating neurodiverse behaviours and the difficulty of the one-size-fits-all school system or the everyone-at-home experience, the soft landing place might well be a lifestyle that you need to adopt for some years. I think the soft landing place is something we evolved when the gap in capacity for us felt continuous.

Then, on very tough days, it was a case of what could be an even softer landing place today?!

PAUSE AND REFLECT

Describe your ideal soft landing place...

. . . .

. . . .

The Centre Line

One of the things I discovered on a run of particularly tough days is how to stay centred. The month before, I'd read somewhere that meditation was good for ADHD brains and had got Wilf to do a 30-day meditation challenge with me. I basically drew a chart and paid him 50p to listen to Jeff Warren, an easy, breezy guy who has ADHD himself, guide us through ten minutes of mindfulness using all sorts of techniques. Every day was a different recording to keep it interesting, and to keep it low-demand I even said that Wilf didn't have to follow the invitations to do this or that on days it felt hard, as long as he took the time to listen along with me anyway. Wilf did every meditation (or listened along), opted for payment in full at the end of the month and hasn't taken up the offer to meditate with me since! I on the other hand got quite into it. Jeff has been a complete lifeline at times, bless him.

On one of the days, Jeff or one of his contemporaries suggested I imagine a centre line running down the middle of my body and into the ground. When I moved, it moved, but it still remained at my centre.

There was something about the feeling of that line, the somatic, embodied experience that resonated with me. I think it spoke to the version of me that was feeling all my children's feelings, that was triggered by their stress. I'm a firm believer, these days, in feeling your feelings rather than soothing, numbing or distracting yourself but... what if you've become so entangled with your child that when they are dysregulated you are pushed off kilter? It's so easy for that to happen.

And then there are the moments that your ADHD child's brain is craving stimulation so much that they poke and prod you, either physically or emotionally, to get your nervous system activated. Yes, that's a thing! Their brains can literally cause drama and upset impulsively because they are craving some dopamine.

Some days I just can't feel my feet on the floor: I'm stressed and I can't get any sense of balance back. It's like my child's nervous system is running the show. When this happens now, I go back to the breath (long, slow out-breaths) and I imagine the feeling of that centre line. I take time to wiggle my toes and sense my feet where they touch the floor.

I've got this down to a fine art. I can get back to centre in a minute or two now, but it used to take a bit longer. Through practice and repetition I've become aware when I'm uncentred or not grounded, and I realign myself, sometimes at regular intervals in the same day because, well, the problems don't just go away! It's become a practice of getting back into my body and being an active operator of my nervous system. My main problem with this technique now is that I forget it exists for weeks at a time. But when I remember, it's super-helpful!

SOMETHING PRACTICAL TO TRY...

Close your eyes. Drop your shoulders, stretch your neck, scrunch and relax your face. Allow yourself to land in this moment. Make the out-breaths a little longer for three to five breaths and then breathe normally.

Then try imagining a centre line running down through your body. You can do this alone, but it could also be a connecting exercise to do with your child, partner or friend.

If you find it hard to get a sense of a centre line: to

start you off, ask someone to draw a line with their finger from the top of your head down past your nose, dropping off at your chin and landing at the top/ middle of your chest and then down to your belly button; or they can go down your back if you prefer.

Imagine it running all the way down the middle of your legs and into the ground. (I find this easier standing up, but you can be sitting or lying too.) Now feel your feet. Are there any sensations there? Are they warm or cold? Tingly? Is there any pain or do they feel relaxed and neutral? Whatever you find, just allow it to be there without trying to change it. Then feel where your feet touch the carpet or hard floor. Try to feel that as much as you can.

You can say something out loud or in your head like, 'I am centred. I am grounded. I ground myself in this moment.'

Imagine how we are made up of millions of moving electrons. (We're not actually solid!) Like a snow globe that's been shaken, our electrons are swirling beyond our physical bodies. Visualize them all being gathered in to your centre line. Your whole body is now the centre line whooshing up from your feet.

Sit or stand with that idea for a moment. Can you keep a sense of it in the back of your mind whilst focusing in on your breathing? Whilst listening to the birds or the kids in the background?

Can you open your eyes and looking down or into the distance still keep a sense of it in your awareness?

Open your eyes when you're done.

Repeat as required – it takes practice (yes, this is sometimes five minutes after the last time).

I ended up making a mini-guided meditation on my voice memos to help me access this line when I was completely dysregulated, and I've since recorded it a little more professionally to help others (it's free on insighttimer.com/LouFearn).

PAUSE AND REFLECT

Try to remember a time recently when you felt grounded and balanced. What did your head, eyes, hands, heart, stomach, legs and feet feel like? When we have a good kinaesthetic (bodily) map of the experience, it's easier to conjure it on demand. For me, 'centred' feels like: a neutral energy in the head, bright behind the eyes, an invisible balancing line down the centre of my body, a warm, calm feeling around my heart and a solid sense of my feet on the floor.

What does it feel like in your body when you are centred?

. . . .
. . . .
. . . .
. . . .
. . . .
. . . .
. . . .
. . . .
. . . .
. . . .
. . . .
. . . .
. . . .

SOMETHING PRACTICAL TO TRY...

Now, here's an extension activity for those who resonate with this. Over the years the kids and I have experimented. A few times we created mini-spa sessions with low lighting and ambient music and took turns to cover each other in blankets and stroke hair and faces. Using beach pebbles, you can add small weights to the centre line when in a lying position – you and your child could do this together if they are interested. Or you can ask a friend or partner to lay them on you.

For extra oomph try doing this on grass or bare ground with your shoes and socks off.

A step further is imagining your chakras. It's not as hippy-dippy as you might think. Our bodies are not actually solid. It's been proved in quantum physics that we are made up of moving atoms. This means that our atom particles are constantly mixing with that of other people's when we come into contact with them. That's a crazy thought, isn't it? It also explains how being in nature is so soothing and energizing. The atomic particles from the plants, trees, river are mixing with ours as we pass by. (Sitting and taking nature in can be more energizing than a brisk walk through it.) Chakras are energy centres, acknowledged by many of the ancient healing traditions, that run up the centre line in your body. Picture each one in turn as balls of coloured energy. You can imagine universal white energy coming from the ground and circling or renewing each chakra. Why not give it a go?

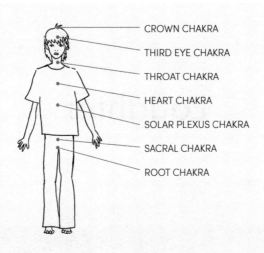

CROWN CHAKRA

THIRD EYE CHAKRA

THROAT CHAKRA

HEART CHAKRA

SOLAR PLEXUS CHAKRA

SACRAL CHAKRA

ROOT CHAKRA

And for women, being pre-menstrual or menopausal can also be ungrounding. Acupuncture and other bodywork treatments can help with this, but if, like me, you can't afford a session, try pinching the space between your big toe and next toe about a centimetre in towards the main part of your foot. Hold the point firmly for 30 seconds and repeat during the day. This is a reflexology point for balancing hormones and PMT symptoms. It's subtle but it works. I've found that it also works on hormonal teenagers – regardless of gender.

Laughter

I think for a long time I forgot to laugh. If I'm completely honest, somewhere along the parenting way I lost myself, my sense of self. I was almost constantly in my stress responses. It got to the point where I found it hard to answer the phone as I was receiving difficult calls every day. I didn't even want to see my extended family or friends because they would all be asking me what I was doing and how things were and I didn't want to feel judged or ashamed, or to have to explain any recent events, which would trigger more stress.

My day was full of holding things together: my paid work, people in my family, the weekly routine, my relationship and my emotions. After years of this I got burnt out. I wasn't sleeping, I had digestive problems, backache from stress, nightmares, social anxiety and fatigue. Both my children were miserable at school and tired and cranky at home. My husband and I were increasingly unable to spend any time together; and when we did, I just worried about the children, or we talked about the current situations they were going through at school or with their friends.

Occasionally I managed to get my head above water. I remember going for a walk on Dartmoor with my two best friends. It was my birthday I think, so I had given myself permission to go out and not feel guilty. We walked, talked, swam in the river and ate a picnic. We listened to what was going on in each other's lives and I joked about all the crazy twists my life had recently taken. We all had a good laugh about that. And it made me remember that I'm funny. I'm not a constant comedian or a quick wit, but I'm a person who notices odd, little, everyday things and points out the funny side to them, and I make my friends laugh.

Driving back, I wasn't sure that my teenage daughter knew I was funny. We definitely didn't laugh much together. I did make my son laugh sometimes. (One of the many positive things he brings to my life is that he laughs heartily at my silliness and encourages a playful side in me.)

The same thing happened a few months later at Christmas when my friends and I went to see a film at the cinema. This time I had brought my daughter along, and I became aware of her watching me, the me that I was with my women friends, a different, lighter version of me that she didn't see at home.

I thought about how, out of the parents and teachers I knew, it was the ones who had a good sense of humour to keep them sane that seemed to be able to balance the children the best. Humour was a release when things got stressful and a useful tool in maintaining rapport with the kids, a light and breezy state to roll things along.

Now I'm not for one minute suggesting you develop a sense of humour, because we are who we are and I'm an intense person most of time. Light-hearted is not something anyone would describe me as. But what I'm learning is that where possible it's good to lean in to your humour and to make as much time for yourself as possible to be around people who bring out the best in you, in even a crazy, busy week. Especially then. Don't wait for Christmas to meet up.

And humour is a good strategy when things go wrong. Not making fun out of each other, never disrespecting your children, but making light of the situation. It's been proven that laughter enhances your intake of oxygen-rich air, stimulates your heart, lungs and muscles and increases endorphins that are released in your brain. It decreases your blood pressure (making you more capable of navigating tricky situations) and can stimulate circulation, aid muscle relaxation and reduce some of the physical symptoms of stress, as well as connecting you with others and helping your mood. Phew! That's a lot of stuff.

Look, it's something I'm definitely still working on and in this vein here are some of the things I've considered:

PAUSE AND REFLECT

Who, outside of your immediate family, does it feel good to spend time with? (Basically, who fills your bucket rather than depleting it?)

. . . .

. . . .

. . . .

. . . .

. . . .

. . . .

. . . .

. . . .

Who makes you laugh or feel lighter?

. . . .

. . . .

. . . .

. . . .

Who do you make laugh?

. . . .

. . . .

. . . .

. . . .

Can you be your true self with this person?

. . . .

. . . .

. . . .

. . . .

SOMETHING PRACTICAL TO TRY...
And now, here's an exercise to try.

Smile.

Yep, I mean right now, sitting in that chair, on that train to work, in a café or lying on the bed, wherever you're reading this. It might be forced, and that's ok. Move your mouth and eyes into a smile. Then, notice how it feels in your head when you do that.

Drop your shoulders down and back a bit to lift your

chest and heart area as if your heart wants to see the sky. How does it feel? Isn't it weird that even when it's forced, our responses are so wired in, that the brain and body subtly react? You can do this at any time of the day for a shift in spirits. I've never told anyone this before, but I've taken in dark moments to looking myself in the mirror, looking myself deep in the eyes and smiling. I say to myself, 'I see you.' And sometimes the mad act of doing this makes me genuinely laugh. At the very least it's another way to connect with yourself. And if you give it a go too, then I won't feel as silly.

- Arrange to see or call the people that make you laugh more regularly. Could you do an evening class/choir/group with them to have the meet-ups more regularly?

- What about creating your own group meet-ups?

I'm sure you know how to meet your own friends if you want to, but when you're tired, big nights out where you all have to dress up or recover from the following day can be off-putting. People often bail. Have you considered the obstacles that put you or other tired parents off? What about a regular coffee time at someone's house, no make-up required, or two hours, early evening, in a friend's garden with an agreed early end time. If it's manageable, you're all the more likely to attend more often. Set an intention to put a few dates in the diary; and if they don't happen, notice why so that you can adapt the plan next time.

PAUSE AND REFLECT

What one thing will you commit to doing this week that might involve laughing with friends? Who would be your most likely partner-in-crime?

. . . .

. . . .

. . . .

. . . .

. . . .

. . . .

. . . .

. . . .

. . . .

. . . .

If you don't have that person in your life right now, keep an eye out for them. Is there an online group or a podcast that makes you giggle and feel part of something?

Not Alone

At one point I was within the very heart of our primary school community. But over time and with mounting difficulties I began to get playground anxiety. Well, all round anxiety really, but particular moments of dread were dropping off a crying, clinging child in front of the other parents whisking in and pecking cheeks and handing over lunch boxes very promptly on their way to important jobs or coffee dates. And worse than that even... the end-of-the-day pickup when everyone gathers to wait.

I'm a prompt person by nature, but I found myself not wanting to talk to the other parents, even those I knew quite well, who would ask how things were going with this or that teacher and tell me about all the clubs, piano exams or extra-curricular activities their child was doing. I wouldn't know what their little darling (or the teacher) had reported back about how my little darling was disrupting the class. I know other mums who also struggled with rejection on behalf of their child when they didn't get invited to parties or return play dates. It feels shameful. And it hurts.

Some of the other children would come out of the classroom clutching artwork, hair clipped back looking the exact same way as when their parents had dropped them off in the morning. My child and a handful of others would either be red-faced in a jumper they didn't want to take off (a firm jumper or sports vest can give good sensory feedback and make them clearer headed) or without a coat in the pelting rain, the teacher shouting over to me that they'd been TOLD to put it on. I think on those days they needed to feel the cold air and the rain on their little faces, to come alive, after all that sitting and the interminable worksheets. Mine chewed his top or the sleeve of his jumper in his attempt to keep himself present. His uniform was wet and full of holes. He was constantly told off for this, despite my explaining that I didn't mind, and it was really the least of everyone's problems. It makes me feel so sad to look back and see with better understanding all the things he was doing to try to cope and how much he was told off by teachers for doing them.

But there is love and understanding to be found in the parents of other neurodiverse children. These people know your pain, your fears, your dreams. They are also in pain in the playground, attending a lot of medical appointments and scrolling through reviews for the best white noise machines, weighted blankets and whatnot. They too scour the lost property for all the lost things. And they are people with whom you can share stories and knowledge. Not only that, but they are often able to support your child for play dates and maybe even sleepovers because they are flexible, ask about food preferences and care that your child feels safe and enjoys themselves. They value your child for who they are and the friendship they bring.

There was a time when I was unwilling to leave my son with anyone except my husband, my mum and the mum of his friend. I barely knew her because we rarely had time for coffee, but I knew enough. I saw how my son was treated by her and how he felt at her house. This woman was pure gold in my life; and when she occasionally asked me to look after her son (outside of the natural invitations), I stepped up for her even when I was tired with a full heart.

When our boys went on a very unsupported residential together, where they weren't allowed to ring home, she was the only person I wanted to speak to.

Other parents in the same situation are magical. Yes, there will be times when your catch-ups are triggering. I don't always have capacity to hear the terrible failures of the system when I'm trying to give myself a break from how it's failing us too. But on the whole, I want to hear what worked for her family because it might work for mine. And I want to hear how she's getting through the week.

And when everything is utterly shit, those are the friends that come round and hug me tight and remind me that this journey is a rollercoaster and tomorrow things will feel different. Tomorrow I might wake up and feel peaceful and content and like I'm nailing it. She knows this because last week she was having a shit day, and I was there to remind her whilst we drank coffee until we felt jittery and beyond.

Friends can help you on your journey to find balance in the home. They can be a fresh perspective, a step back from all the emotions. They can feel like a strong, supportive presence backing you up just by existing in your contacts list. You can offer each other respite in the form of childcare and peace from knowing you are in the thick of life together. They can remind you to see the funny side, be there to hug you when things go wrong and celebrate all the mini-milestones that wouldn't matter to anyone else. They are the people you can suffer and laugh with through a crappy attempt at a day out at the beach, where for reasons known and unknown none of the kids enjoys themselves!

They are the antidote to all the feelings that happy-family, social media posts stir up. Do you know the ones I mean? The back-to-school posts when your child is miserable or refusing, the holding of certificates when yours is struggling to learn the basics, the fun but relaxing holiday snaps when your own family is bickering, or someone won't get out of the car.

In my friendship group we've got kids who hate busy places, won't stand on the sand, can't wear a wetsuit, are phobic about seagulls or dogs or rain or the chance of rain and those who won't be photographed. The shiny posts of others can make you feel quite depressed and lacking if your family life looks very different, but I think a good friend in a similar situation normalizes your own life experience.

PAUSE AND REFLECT

Imagine having a kid's beach bucket that you carried around with you half full of water. Which friends and family members (extended family – not the one you've created) add to your bucket and which take away from it?

The people who add to my bucket when I see them are...

....

....

....

....

The people who take from my bucket are...

....

....

....

....

It makes sense to spend more time in your week and month with the people in your life who add to your bucket. They feel like a relief to be around, and hopefully you add to theirs too. Avoid people who only take from your bucket or limit the time you spend with them especially when you're running at full capacity. (Also be wary of people who pour so much into your bucket that the water is overflowing and running down the sides. Those are people with whom you need to set firmer boundaries.)

PAUSE AND REFLECT

If you don't have friends with neurodiverse children, how could you look out for and reach out to those who live near to you? List one step below that you're going to take next to make that happen.

. . . .

. . . .

. . . .

. . . .

. . . .

. . . .

. . . .

. . . .

I met one friend by noticing her kid was similar and asking in the playground if she wanted to get a coffee someday, even though her son was two years above and she didn't know who I was! Sleep deprived and burnt out, she was so surprised by my directness that she gave me her number. I was worried that she might not want to meet up but forced myself to message anyway, to be vulnerable to rejection. It took a bit of sorting because... well school runs aren't easy for either of us, but in the end we had that coffee and it turned out that she was also struggling, had become socially anxious and was in need of a friend. Our children don't hang out. They are too similar, but that's ok, we understand.

Others I met on a local parenting course. There are also local in-person support groups that meet up regularly and Facebook groups. And friends with kids usually know of other friends in similar situations.

If you can, open yourself up to rejection. It isn't about you. Some people are just not in the mental space where they can be a new friend in this moment in time. Keep on being brave, asking and exploring until you find your people.

And if you just can't, right now, do any of that, please know that that is very ok too. You might be feeling a bit raw or not have the opportunities to get out and meet new people or the capacity to maintain even existing friendships. Are you able to connect with others online or join a podcast community? Even books, like this one, can be a very connecting experience and make us feel that little bit safer in the world.

PART TWO

Rebuilding your sense of self

Self-Care (and I don't mean face masks)

'Put on your own oxygen mask first!' Oof! How I came to eventually hate that well-trodden phrase. What exactly does it mean for starters? What does an 'oxygen mask' look like in the real-life situation in my house? And who the 'bleep' is giving them out?

Face masks and scented candles are pleasant, but when I talk about self-care, I'm talking about being still for just a minute and listening to your body. What does your body need to feel ok, right now, in this moment? So often we don't know, and we don't take the time to work it out. We grab at the first thought. I should want this or I should do that. The body holds the truth.

If the first thought says Haribo or alcohol or phone scrolling, dig deeper. Ask yourself, 'If my brain says it wants a glass of wine, what does my body really want? What's the desire beneath that?'

And I'm not in any way saying you can't have that glass of wine. Have it. But as you're pouring it or sipping it, take the time to know what your body really wanted. Spoiler alert: It wasn't wine – 100% of the time.

I once thought I wanted some of my son's Haribo sours. They don't sit well in my middle-aged tummy, but my brain still insisted it wanted them. I ate one. Five minutes later I went back for another. 'What is this all about?' I asked myself. (I talk to myself a lot!) 'What are you really wanting?' After five Haribo sour forays, it turned out that I really wanted sugar and the sour taste on my tongue. 'But why?' I continued to explore. It seemed that I wanted to perk myself up and it was too late in the day for me to have a coffee. I kept going with my investigation. 'Why do you need to perk yourself up?' I knew immediately. I was very tired as I wasn't sleeping. So why didn't I just take a nap? I knew that too. Because it was Wilf's birthday and I'd persuaded his dad to take him and his mate out to do an activity whilst I got the food together. I could have rested for 20 minutes but I felt too guilty when my husband (also tired) was holding things together. What my body really needed was rest.

Another thing I do is crave an ice lolly when I really want a glass of water, and I've noticed Wilf goes for the frozen fruit and ice poles a lot. Now, when either of us does that, we grab a glass of water first.

When we need hydrating, we can *think* we want an ice lolly or a starburst or an apple; and when we want rest, sometimes our brains reach for Haribo or coffee or sugary snacks. Self-care is getting to the bottom of what your core needs actually are and addressing them.

Not long after the Haribo incident, I made a list of needs and things I typically do to half fulfil them, seeing how each one missed the mark. A crazy one was if I was feeling stressed about how Wilf's school day was going, I would go online or to a store and buy him outdoor equipment. Things like walking boots, waterproof trousers, etc. He used to do a lot of that Forest School stuff rain or shine, and so I was always trying to buy layers of protection and comfort for him. I once bought snow trousers in the sale three years running, and it didn't snow for any of those winters; the kids found them still with their labels on and laughed their socks off. It's a family joke now.

Eating food that you don't really want when you're not hungry, drinking alcohol, buying clothes, shopping of any kind (including books you don't read and online courses you don't attend): it's all semi-invisible, subtle self-medicating. It makes things feel more under control, and possibly a teeny tiny bit better for a fraction of a moment, but it doesn't really reach the spots. It can make you feel better in the short term, in a kind of numb way, but then the same or worse afterwards. That's how you know it's not a real act of care. It's not actually caring for yourself because it's not bringing you back to life or soothing you or doing any of the things you unconsciously hope it will do.

The left column of the table below lists the mad, half-arsed things I do that are just enough to stop me really attending to the need but also don't fully satisfy my need either. Glennon Doyle, author of *Untamed* and co-host of the *We Can Do Hard Things* podcast, calls these 'the easy button'. I thought about all the things I fill my day and week with. On the right are the core needs I've discovered underneath the surface desires. I had to really dip down into myself over a few days to ponder what these were. These same actions may have different needs beneath them for you. It's a very individual thing. I invite you to make similar lists for yourself.

Half-arsed attempts at meeting my needs (the easy button)	Core need
Eating chocolate (without tasting or enjoying it)	Wanting comfort/nurturing/ to numb emotions, needing energy/sensory input
Eating crisps	Wanting stress relief/to self-soothe, needing energy
Drinking coffee (personally never giving this up)	Feeling tired or dull/joyless

Drinking alcohol	To wind down or pep up and be fun, to give myself a treat, to take the edge off my suffering
Wanting an ice lolly, fruit or fruity sweets	Needing a glass of water or tired and needing a rest
Shopping online for my children	Wanting control/to protect or prepare them/to feel on top of their mental health states
Shopping online for myself – for comforting or energizing clothes, craft supplies that I never get round to using	Wanting to feel better emotionally and be prepared/capable/confident/creative
Tidying house	Wanting to feel in control/at peace
Painting rooms or furniture	Wanting an environment that brings me to life or soothes me
Scrolling Instagram	Wanting connection or to feel inspired/alive, wanting comfort and nature
Watching TV – rubbish stuff I'm not even enjoying sometimes	Wanting headspace/distraction/stress release, exploring interests to bring me to life
Going into town or browsing the home section of the supermarket	Wanting space/time alone/to be outside in nature
Doing crossword puzzle, Wordfeud	Wanting time to myself/a distraction from a stressful situation, making easy connection/repair with my partner (as we do it together)

When you start to make these lists, you may not know what unfulfilling actions you do or what the core needs beneath them are. But the act of making the lists means you'll start to question it all and notice.

The next step is to make a list of essential needs. If you didn't have a care in the world or any responsibilities, what would you regularly need to stay balanced?

Your needs will be individual to you, but to get you thinking I'm sharing a list of needs that I have come up with. When I translated all the things I do on the regular and looked at what was beneath these actions they sort of fell roughly into these categories. I can't always attend to all my needs but knowing what they are and voicing them is a crucial first step to recovering your sense of self. (This is an ongoing list that I'm still adding to:)

- comfort/nurturing

- connection (intimacy, honest conversations, warm friendships)

- to be financially, physically and emotionally safe/secure

- to feel on top of my children's mental health

- to feel in control

- to be alive, joyful, have meaning in my life (to be creative)

- time alone

- stillness/to spend time in nature

- to explore my own interests

- sensory input/movement

- to feel energized

- rest and time to look after my body

- to feel at peace

- to relieve stress

- a minute to take a breath and centre myself

- to love myself.

This led me to think about what hits the spot for me in addressing these needs. Again, it will be different for you, but mine might be a helpful starting point. For example, *when I need comfort…* I now know that what I really need is soft clothing in dark colours, a hot water bottle, a hug if available, hot drinks, homemade soup, lying down in my bed, going for a walk, seeing a close friend. And *when I need peace of mind and stress release*... I take a walk in nature, but it has to be visibly green (not the seaside – for others out there it might be the seaside, but for me it's green canopies of trees over my head). Wide open spaces also help my brain feel clear – with an endless view, no clutter, no houses in the distance. The moor is my favourite place, pure nature for miles in every direction and wooded moments too.

I'm in the middle of making my own list of things that genuinely soothe, calm or invigorate me. It's an ongoing exploration, but the table below lists what I've got so far.

Actual self-care	Core need
Hot water bottle, rocking myself, soft clothes in dark colours, reading in bed, a meditation, homemade soup, a hot drink, a healthy lunch, an afternoon on the sofa, a woodland walk, seeing a close friend, writing a kind and loving note to myself	Comfort/nurturing/ learning to love myself
Swimming in cold water (rivers and the sea), a warm bath with essential oils, meditation or breathwork, reflexology points on feet, crunchy salty foods, a walk with an open view, music that hits the spot or silence, alone time	Stress relief/ self-soothing

Learning something new; following my curiosity down some rabbit hole; exploring somewhere new – going to a town or village I haven't been to before and looking at the narrow cobbled streets and colourfully painted front doors, maybe popping into a charity shop; checking out a new café or a new trail; going to a new friend's house (I love getting inspired to do creative stuff in my home); crafting (a big tick box for me especially if it's all laid out and simple) – like a friend hosting a craft session is amazing, or paying to go on a craft workshop session; evening classes (can be tiring, but if they fully excite you they can be energizing); any small creative activity, like painting a picture or collaging (and not for the end product – I'm not an artist!); a kitchen dance about, a dance class, a karaoke sesh whilst I'm cooking dinner; being in nature; gathering and foraging – pinecones for kindling or hedgerow berries for a crumble (never fails to tune me back in to a childlike sense of wonder)	To feel alive and joyful when feeling tired or dead inside
Warm shower, coconut oil on dry areas, a few yoga bedtime stretches for my achy back, reflexology points on feet for back and stress levels, lavender rollerball on wrist, guided meditation	To wind down before bed
A short burst of conscious connection with each child, meeting them where they are emotionally and in their areas of interest	To feel on top of my children's mental health

cont.

Actual self-care	Core need
Self-care (see wind down before bed); making the time to create a nourishing meal I actually feel like eating; tidying a small area where I can sit and relax; making a list of things I have to do and identifying the priorities, then deciding on one thing I'll definitely do today; a haircut	To feel more in control
Finding a friend who's available for a coffee or walk right now; sending messages to other friends; having some authentic conversations; asking for a hug; planning a meal to share with someone I love	Connection
A walk, run or swim; music or podcast in headphones; a cup of tea in the garden; singing loudly on my own in the car; going for a drive with a flask of coffee and drinking it somewhere with a great view; reading a book; doing a meditation (this can be done in a parked car in your drive if you can't leave your children!)	Space, time alone, to be outside in nature

PAUSE AND REFLECT

Begin to think about what would be on your list and start to try these out. Do they hit the spot? How do you know? Take some time to do this before you move on with the journal.

It may help to reflect on what you enjoyed doing as a child and then before you had children.

As I child I enjoyed doing...

....
....
....
....

Before having kids, I enjoyed...

....
....
....
....

These days the things that soothe me are...

....
....
....
....

Some things that bring me to life are...

....
....
....
....

Now take the time to look at your own core needs. Start with my bulleted list and add any more you think of as you go along. If time, money and space were no object, what would you need each day and each week to feel good?

When you've done this consider whether any of my self-care ideas and activities feel true for you. Note them down and try them out. Do they lead you to more specific ideas of your own? Keep adding what you find out to your own list until you've narrowed it down like me.

And if you don't know yet what your core needs are, just consider each point on the bulleted list as a starting point. You could also add a number out of 5 beside each one to see which are the strongest needs right now (0 being no real need detected, 1 being a mild sense of a need and 5 being 'I strongly need to prioritize this right now').

The Self-Compassion Bangle

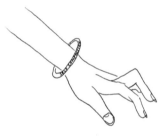

When things go wrong at home, I sometimes feel like I'm failing. I look at all my flaws and weaknesses and feel rubbish.

There was a time when I scrolled down social media posts from families I know, looking at the highlights of their days out, their wholesome family lives, and hated how difficult ours were in comparison. On holiday, all our needs and personalities conflicted, and with less space and all the tiring transitions, it was harder than being at home.

I know now not to believe the hand-picked, glossy photos. Most of us can conjure a few seconds that look good to the outside world if we put our minds to it. The truth is there are good days and bad days. Easier parts to a hard day and harder parts to an easy day. Coming off social media can help. That's what many parents of neurodiverse kids do. It might be worth trying it for a month and seeing the difference, or muting people you know who trigger you.

They say 'comparison is the thief of joy', and it really is. No good comes out of comparing your child with others in their peer group or your family life to that of others you know. Author Byron Katie says, 'Stay in your own business,' and that has become one of a few mantras that has settled within me, something I pull out time and time again. When you stop comparing, you stop obsessing about what you or your child lacks, where you all fall short, and this naturally allows more focus on what you're all actually doing individually and as a family. There is so much more peace to be found in that.

Your friend's child is doing a billion GCSEs? Great. That's their business. Another is cooking a meal for the family one night a week, whilst holding down a part-time job, full-time study and putting away their laundry? How lovely. Not your business. A kid in your child's class is baking cakes for charity and all your friends are running a half marathon? Fab. That's their business. Stay firmly in yours. Stay in your own business. Perhaps you don't feel well today and you're bundled up on the sofa watching your kid watch TV whilst all this baking and marathon running and putting away of laundry is happening. That sofa is your only business, along with listening to what your body needs to get well and what your child needs to stay balanced and entertained whilst you heal.

How we talk to ourselves is important. I have this little mini-notebook next to my bed. It's small and chunky and I scribble a few sentences on each page when I feel like it, mostly ignoring the lines. It's been LIFE CHANGING. The words are written to myself in the voice that a kind parent would speak to her beloved child to soothe them. Some days it just says 'I love you' or 'You've got this'. It really doesn't matter if that's all you write on every page. The stuff I write can be quite general like that and often repetitive, because I like to hear the same things said over and over to me. But there are also days when I get more specific.

When I'm feeling low, I lie down on my bed and flick through those pages. Although my brain knows I wrote them to myself, it doesn't matter; it's weirdly just as soothing as if someone else said them. They are verbal hugs and have helped me to cultivate a kind and loving inner voice I can draw on when things get hard.

After all, who are you for your child or a friend in need? I bet you're kind, loving, capable, protective and soothing towards them, especially when you can see that they're struggling. One of the ways into finding this compassionate voice is to imagine coming across your child or a friend you love who is feeling the same as you are now. How would you speak soothingly to them? At first imagine it is them, sobbing, you're talking to. You'd say something along the lines of, 'It's alright my love, I'm right here. I'm here, sweetheart. You're not alone in this. I'm always going to have your back.' Say it out loud, how you would say it.

Then swap the image of your child/friend in your mind to *you* and say the same things. Notice how it feels.

You are ALL those things for your children and others around you. It's a part of your self. Why not be that person for the more overwhelmed vulnerable part of you?

When my dad died unexpectedly, I realized how I hadn't just lost my dad, I'd lost a kind and loving voice that cared about boring stuff I had going on that no one else wanted to hear! He was a cheerleader for me, always believing I was successful as a human even when I did nothing but show up.

Over the next few years after he'd gone, I had to learn to become that person for myself. We all did. My mum, my brother and me. We heard his voice in our ears. We talked to him. We tried to be that presence for each other, but in the end, we all had to become that voice for ourselves.

Since losing my dad, it's made me realize that I have pockets of validation, love and compassion stowed everywhere outside of me, in my husband, my mum, brother and different friends. I would be having a difficult day and I'd want to reach out, but when people were unavailable or part of me didn't want to make contact for a whole host of reasons, I was forced to step up and be that person for myself.

The parent in me had to soothe the scared or overwhelmed child part within me. And when it did, it allowed my brain to see the child part as just a part. Moments before, I *was* my fear and vulnerability, during those times when my anxious child part was running the show. That one part felt like all of me. But when a more resourced part of me stepped in to comfort, I could see there were many parts of me and glimpse my true self, the core soul self beyond all emotions and behaviours. It was peaceful.

I've since found out that this is actually a valid therapeutic approach known as the Internal Family Systems model, created by Richard Schwartz in the 1980s.

Nowadays if I breathe and write myself a note, do a meditation, write in my journal and offer myself a soft landing place, then I can do a really good job of soothing myself, and I feel more empowered for doing it because I'm always available, never going to die (until I do) and always know exactly what I need to hear. When I look outside of myself for support, I sometimes feel: lonely or rejected (if people are busy); young and fearful that it would one day not be there (having experienced my dad dying); too much of a burden, too needy, leaving me at risk of being misunderstood and left wanting (if friends don't quite get it right). Seeing myself as my greatest support and resource made me feel steadier in the world. That silly little chunk of a notebook by my bed empowers me like nothing else.

I feel afraid or in need of support → I soothe myself and recognize the adult part of my capital-S Self that is grounded and capable → My grounded adult Self comforts the scared childlike part within me → I feel cared for, empowered and at peace.

Inspired by Elizabeth Gilbert, who taught me about writing to soothe myself, I now wear a bangle with 'I'm right here' engraved on it, another holy mantra for me that reminds me I can be there for myself. (Liz writes daily letters in her journal to Unconditional Love and Unconditional Love writes back its reply through Liz. It's a way of accessing her unconscious, higher self and loving herself just as she is in words she longs to hear. If you'd like to know more about this soulful, self-love practice you can find everything on the Substack app if you pop her name in the search bar.) Liz herself, of course, gets her mantras tattooed on because she's wild (in the best sense of that word, as in closer to self) and adventurous and much braver than me. I'm building up to this, but my mantras change as I try this one and that one for size, so it's a bangle for me as I write this!

Mantras are a short pithy phrase that reaches you on a deeper level. They feel universally true and during stressful situations when it's hard to think straight, a memorable mantra can be a real guiding light. My favourite mantras currently are:

- Stay in your own business.

- I'm right here.

- That's not my circus.

PAUSE AND REFLECT

What would be a useful mantra for you?

. . . .

. . . .

. . . .

. . . .

Can you do something creative with that? (Doodle it in your journal, paint a picture for your wall or create something on the computer using a font you like. Embroider it on a cushion, get it printed on a mug, a t-shirt or etched on a bangle.)

What advice would you give the adult version of your son or daughter if they were in your situation right now?

. . . .

. . . .

. . . .

. . . .

How would you tell them that you love them and they're doing great, they're doing their best?

. . . .

. . . .

....

....

Read out those words to yourself. Say them a few times until you can fully soak them in and believe them. Then start a journal or small book of comforting words. Leave it by your bed with a pen and write what you need to hear in difficult moments.

....

....

....

....

....

....

....

....

Energy from Play

You may be thinking, 'God, if I had the time and money to go and play, I would not be sitting here trying to restore my sanity with a wellbeing journal.' I hear you. But what I have noticed is that when I make time to play, I come back with energy to SPARE. True fact.

It turns out that play is a major source of energy. If you think about it, there's a lot of output as a parent. But what is going in to fuel it all? Food and sleep. Yes. Hopefully. But that's not enough. If you're living off food and sleep, chances are you are walking around self-medicating with coffee and alcohol and online shopping, and none of it is hitting the spot. I've been there, and still am at times.

So, what does play look like for adults? Brené Brown says that it's doing activities that aren't in themselves productive. You're doing them for the act of doing something pleasurable, not the end product. Crocheting a blanket for a friend's new baby is not play, even if you love crocheting, because there's a timeline, an expectation (even if it's just yours), and you're doing something for the purpose of having a product to give to a friend. Running a marathon is not play either. It's goal-oriented.

Play is the sort of activity where you get engrossed and lose track of time. And as you're doing the thing, you feel a sense of peace, liberated, uninhibited, satisfied, bright, alive or curious. Brené describes the energy that you get from adrenaline as being akin to the rush after eating a donut. But the energy that you get from play is more like a green smoothie feeling.

Play gives you what you need to cope with the other areas of your life and keeps you in loving relationship with your family.

It's so different for everyone, and something I have noticed over the years is that some people view sport and craft as wholesome play and gaming and TV as a lazy attempt at play. This adds a layer of shame for those who love those things and takes away some of the benefits that those people get from their play time. Gaming (especially with friends) and TV are totally legit if you've tried the other things, and they don't feel fun and all-consuming. They are not so legit when you're just watching or playing any old thing that doesn't bring you alive and feel satisfying.

It's possible that we get stuck in a rut. We keep doing the thing we've always done and so miss out on discovering new things that could bring us back to life. It's good to have those people in your life who invite in the new so that you can learn more about what you like and don't like and add things to your play list.

For me, playing looks like: dancing about at home, singing, creating playlists, crafting, sewing, dying fabric, reading, painting, collaging, walks on the moor, foraging, collecting pinecones for kindling, picnics with friends, binge watching a series I'm totally into, coffee with a view, bodyboarding, night walks, Greek island hopping, mountain views, reading novels, writing stories, feeding birds and my guilty pleasure... watching animal rescue videos.

For my husband, playing looks like: surfing, building a surfboard from scratch, listening to music, an occasional noodling on his guitar, playing online chess and word games, playing pool, firepits, a coffee overlooking the water.

PAUSE AND REFLECT

What does playing look like to you?

. . . .

. . . .

. . . .

. . . .

On my list (above) there are definitely things I haven't done in ages despite enjoying them. I've done nothing from the list in the last two weeks. Instead, I've done a few local walks, met friends for coffee and watched bad TV. It's something to be mindful of and check in on regularly.

PAUSE AND REFLECT

What really fills you up with light? How are you going to get some of that into each day/week?

. . . .

. . . .

. . . .

. . . .

. . . .

. . . .

. . . .

. . . .

. . . .

Selfishness vs. Starved of Self

There comes a point, probably when you mention wanting to do something on your own or with friends and then you mention wanting to do another thing straight after, that your partner will start to baulk at the situation, because when you take time to attend to your needs and have some fun, they have to carry the weight of the responsibilities at home.

It may be your overburdened friends who bring some sort of judgement to your doorstep, or your mum who always had to be selfless, or your kids who want you around. It may be your own self-worth that gets in your way. However, you got into the situation of never giving yourself a moment; the minute your liberation affects others, they will have opinions about it and how much time you can take.

What is the line between meeting your own needs and filling your bucket to refuel yourself and being selfish?

Oprah's life coach, Martha Beck, who's written a brilliant book called, *The Way of Integrity*, says that 'selfishness is definitely a thing, and it happens when someone is starved of self'.

Did you hear that? It literally only occurs when a person has been starved of self. When they've had to put all their energy into responding to others.

'If someone holds a pillow over your face, you are thinking only about breath, but if you are able to breathe freely, you don't think about it at all,' she explains. And when we come across a 'selfish' person, who feels mean and toxic in that self-ishness, you can be guaranteed that that person's self is being stifled to the point where they cannot think about anything else. They've been robbed of their true selves. Separation from self is unbearable, and the resentment just grows and grows.

That's something to think about. I'm pretty sure most parents are starved of self because daily life so often takes all our time and energy, leaving nothing for play and self-care.

Martha recommends that your priority in this situation is to put a lot of your energy into understanding who you are and what it takes for you to be happy. 'It's a recovery period for the self and every time you give yourself something it genuinely needs, you'll notice that you'll feel a little more energetic towards others.' When you step too far and push for too much it won't feel good to you because that's not in our true nature. You'll naturally think, I was out a bit too much this week, so I'll make space for connected family time or make sure my partner has time off to keep the balance.

To reconnect with self, you need to ask yourself some questions.

PAUSE AND REFLECT

What feels warm, free and joyful right now? (Look at what you identified as play in the last chapter – what feels like a warm thing to do today or this week?)

. . . .

. . . .

. . . .

. . . .

What friendships feel warm?

. . . .

....

....

....

What activity feels joyful and freeing?

....

....

....

....

What can I add to my day today that feels like peace and
a relief?

....

....

....

....

I used to think that I could get to myself at the end of the
list. If I did everything for everyone else first, then I could
tick my box afterwards, but that meant that the energy with
which I was doing things for other people was actually angry
energy, and tired and exhausted energy... let's face it, it's easy
to run out of steam and not get to our thing. I started out only
being able to write fiction when everyone was happy and fed
and the house was tidy and everything under the sun had

been done. Of course, I rarely got to it; and when I did, I was exhausted. Early on in our family life my husband told me that I didn't have time to write. If I'd done everything else, I needed to help earn some money.

Eventually I wrote down a list of everything I hated about my life and everything I loved to do and wished was part of my week. I asked myself, what one thing from the wish list would make all the to-do list bearable? It was having time to write.

So, I went to bed early, set my alarm and crept out into the garden office before anyone woke up to write for several hours. Sometimes I didn't write. I was too tired to think straight at silly o'clock in the morning, but I still got up, made coffee and went out there. I did a meditation, wrote in my diary, watched interviews with famous authors. When I couldn't write I was building stamina to function at that time in the morning and I filled my bucket in other ways. It wasn't always easy to get up, but I have never once regretted it. It's a magical time in the day that fills me up and gives me the energy I need for the day ahead.

A Chat with Fear

You might have heard the saying 'A life lived in fear is a life half lived'. It comes from the film *Strictly Ballroom* written and directed by Baz Luhrmann. One of the things that holds us back from stepping out of cultural norms and following our instincts to find the right sort of life for us and our children is fear. It's also sometimes fear that stops us being creative and doesn't allow us to play.

Fear lurks. You can't quite feel the shape of it, but it can step in when you try to change things up. It could be a feeling in your stomach, in your chest or somewhere else in your body. It could be a million thoughts or a voice inside your head.

What if I'm a bad parent? What if I'm making the wrong choices for my child or for us as a family? What if I'm getting this all wrong? I can't play because I can't leave them. I can't take my eye off the ball. I'm the only one who can hold this. What if my being away for a few hours makes them more anxious? What if they self-harm or feel suicidal? What if they don't eat all day or forget to drink water? What if they hate me for not being there overnight? What if it's all harder when I get back and not worth it? What if my partner judges me for wanting the luxury of time off when they are busy and overwhelmed too? Is it princessy to want to go dancing or write a book when your family is in crisis? How will the extended family react if I take my child out of school and they don't take any GCSEs?

All fears I have had at some point or another.

Elizabeth Gilbert wrote an amazing book called *Big Magic*. It's a book about tuning into your creative, playful side despite your fear of failure or not being good enough. I read it years ago when I was scared to write a novel and I wholly recommend it. I didn't know I was scared. I thought I was unmotivated and stuck. But actually, I was frozen in fear. What if it wasn't good enough and never got published? What if everyone saw me trying and then I didn't succeed? But *Big Magic* is more than a book for writer's block. You don't even have to be someone wanting to write a book to benefit from it. It's a recipe for living life fully.

Liz points out that fear doesn't need you to change your

life around it. It just wants to be heard. Its job is to evaluate every risk and let you know what they are. And once it's done its job, it quietens, and you get to choose with your higher consciousness whether you are willing to take those risks.

The next thing to do is for you to write a letter from your Fear. It's a great exercise for people who are creatively stuck, but it's also genius for us parents in a pickle.

According to Liz, this list of things your Fear wants to tell you will not be infinite. You'll find it doesn't take that long to write. When you don't fight fear or interrupt it, it usually only has a few things to tell you. Mine are:

- that I'm afraid of being judged

- that I'm afraid of being a bad parent

- that I'm afraid of getting things wrong

- that I'm afraid of not doing enough, being enough

- that I'm afraid of looking silly

- that I'm afraid to show what I long for, etc.

PAUSE AND REFLECT

Start your letter...

Dear [insert your own name],

I am your Fear, and this is what I want to tell you...

....

....

....

....

....

....

....

....

Write it in one go without too much thought. Just put pen to paper and see what comes out. Keep going until Fear has nothing left to say.

Read your letter through. Consider what Fear has said. Then consider what the cost is to you personally if you don't take the risks. Because when we choose not to do something there is always a cost, the suffering around the thing we are giving up.

For example, when Fear says you must not go out for the evening because it will cause an upset and make everyone in the house miserable, yes that might be true. Your partner, mum or long-suffering babysitter may have it tough for a few hours. The kids may feel highly anxious and act out. It may be uncomfortable for everyone involved and it may be hard for you when you re-enter the fray because everyone may or may not be overtired, not sleeping and dysregulated. All those are risks for some parents. But... what are you personally losing if you don't go out to play? Is it:

- your freedom

- your sense of self

- the relief of not being responsible for a moment

- the chance to play, to explore interests

- the perspective of being away from the household temporarily

- a freshness that gives you more capacity to come back, and love and support

- a chance to connect with your friends (or self)

- a step towards feeling alive and not dead inside

- a chance for your people to practise seeing that their world does not collapse when you are not present for a few hours (empowering them).

When it's listed out it's easy to see that there's more to lose than you first think. And then there are the ongoing losses. If you don't set the precedent of going out tonight, you will also be losing the chance for everyone to grow in a healthy direction that lets all its family members get needs met.

Liz suggests you write back a respectful response to Fear from your wisest self: Dearest Fear...

- Acknowledge your fears and how Fear is just trying to protect you.

- But let Fear know that although it is welcome, it will not be making any decisions for you.

- Your Soul (highest self), Creativity, Inspiration and Wisdom will all be taking turns in the driving seat. Fear can sit in the back and mutter. It is a valued member of the team, but, as Liz says, on the road trip of life it never gets to hold the map, tune the radio or drive the car.

Liz appears to me to be an awakened woman: someone that has stepped out of society's expectations and worked hard to get to the bottom of their original wounding (the wounds that come from our childhood strategies to get, and keep getting, our needs met by our caregivers and, later on, by our partners, friends and family).

When you are able to clearly see that you are being hurt by your own historic wounds or someone else's, and see that in the moment it's happening, you are no longer reacting by lashing back out and inflicting that hurt on others around you. It takes time and effort. It is a breaking of the cycle of generational pain. Because of this, Liz shines brightly and we'll also be hearing from her in the next chapter.

The Permission Slip

Shining a light on and listening to your fears is a crucial step, as was digging deep and excavating your true needs. You're getting somewhere! If you have an inkling of what play looks like to you, that's even more glorious, but as I've discovered, knowing all this and acting on it seem to be two different problems.

My friends and I would talk for hours about self-care, and we really drilled down to the bottom of that, but when we got to all the good stuff we needed in our lives, we noticed that we just weren't doing much about it all.

And fair enough, as I have already told you, we are all up to our ears in it most days, which feels like one step from a nervous breakdown sometimes. But when I spoke to both men and women around me who understood their needs and weren't addressing them, all of them admitted that they found it hard to voice their needs either aloud to themselves or to their partner. They couldn't give themselves permission to meet their needs.

And if their needs conflicted with other family members? They tended to meet other people's needs first and just feel resentful. That is something I'm very guilty of. I'd rather not disappoint my mum, my husband or children so I disappoint myself instead time after time. And I don't do this quietly and gracefully. Nope. The resentment leaks out of me. You can see it on my face, feel it in my prickly energy. I'm like a grumpy teenager.

What is that all about?

Some of you may have grown up in a family where the children fitted around the adults. Your needs were not considered priorities. Others with dysfunctional parental relationships were emotionally neglected. You learned early on that your needs would not be met, and it was less disappointing if you didn't have any. Kids from big families often didn't get as many needs met due to the amount of people in the house and the workload the parents were keeping up with. Some of us probably had selfless mothers who put everyone else first and we've automatically replicated that in own family life. Some family cultures teach you to get up, despite how ill you feel, pull your socks up, put your best foot forward and keep going no matter what. Push through. Those are the kids with 100% attendance at school because they were never allowed a day off. They were taught to ignore their body's cry for rest. Illness is seen as weakness and failure in some families. Or maybe you simply came from a family that watched TV and ate snacks and never explored what might reach their soul.

It doesn't really matter. There are probably a gazillion other reasons why we shut down attending to ourselves, but whatever the reason it ended in low self-worth.

Low self-worth isn't always easy to spot. We tell ourselves we don't have the time to do the things we want to do. Or we don't have the money. Or we might embarrass ourselves trying to do something new. If we don't tell ourselves these things, we might either hear them from people we love who struggle themselves in the same way and bring that shit to our door, or assume that they will tell us these things and imagine the shame if we dare to voice our longings.

Many people struggle with low self-worth and many people live relatively normal lives around it. But low self-worth is the reason people don't give themselves permission to voice their needs and meet their own needs and play. It requires a sense of entitlement and I hope that through your journalling you'll be able to start voicing your needs with confidence. (Entitlement is a word that's somehow become stigmatized and used to describe rich kids that expect the world to deliver everything they desire instantly; I mean it in the traditional sense of simply being allowed.)

I think self-worth is a biggy. Something to delve into and spend time on. Therapy can help. And meditation. There are lots of free self-worth and loving kindness meditations out there.

But in the meantime, here's a few things that have guided me in the right direction:

- Knowing that my kids are unconsciously watching what I do, the choices I make for myself and then building their map of adult life based on that. This helps me to choose a pathway that's liberating for all of us. They may not like it when I choose me. They will probably complain when I get ready to go out or my attention's on gluing and sticking a collage at the dining room table, but I can rest easy in my mind knowing that this is right for all of us.

- In Glennon Doyle's book *Untamed: Stop Pleasing, Start Living*, she says: 'Every time you're given a choice between disappointing someone else and disappointing yourself, your duty is to disappoint that someone else. Your job throughout your entire life, is to disappoint as many people as it takes to avoid disappointing yourself.' Life is short and precious and when we're pleasing our families of origin or our partners and children and not meeting our own truth, our own needs, we're wasting it. Other people seeing our longings make us feel vulnerable, but that doesn't mean we shouldn't air them. The way to fulfilment is to feel that awkwardness, that vulnerability and fear of judgement and just keep going towards the thing you long for anyway because if you don't, you are just walking through your life dead inside, which is no good to anyone.

- Elizabeth Gilbert's Letter to Fear.

- Elizabeth Gilbert's Permission Slip (see later).

In *Big Magic*, Liz Gilbert says we all come from makers, ancestors who created things, even if that wasn't apparent in our parents' generation. Humans have a natural impulse to create and make things more beautiful than they need to be to function, like a carved chair for example. It doesn't need to be carved or decorated to form a seat, but someone made it that way because they wanted to, because it brought them joy or satisfaction to create it that way. She describes how we are all creative beings. It's in us even if we've just been sat on the sofa snacking all this time. It's part of the human experience, and yet many of us are scared to allocate time from a squeezed schedule on it. This is even more the case for frazzled parents. One of the fears is that if we do something that is no use to anyone else, that no one needs, that no one asked for, that doesn't have a great end result, or that doesn't make money or help anyone in any way, then we have wasted our precious time. That is the voice of fear.

And fear comes from a different part of your brain. It doesn't understand creativity and play. It's old and reptilian. It was in our brains before humans evolved a creative response. And it doesn't reward you in the way that our culture teaches us is worthy.

Liz lists many reasons to create stuff, but the ones that stuck with me as a struggling parent were: 'You do it to remind yourself that you are not just here to pay bills and die. You do it because you want to be a participant in your life.' Because our minds need stretching to feel healthy. Because we want to be a main character in our own lives. Because we need creative activity to stop us going crazy. And lastly because regardless of what the outcome is, you will be full up inside and lighter and brighter for it. You'll be a better person for it and therefore better able to parent.

And I've noticed this to be true. When I schedule time with friends and I go off to sit around a firepit by the sea or for a river swim and picnic or to see a film at the cinema or allow myself to create something, I'm different when I return. It doesn't matter how tiring my activity was, I come back somehow shiny and with far more capacity to cope with everything I meet back at the ranch.

'And what's the alternative to doing it?' Liz asks in her 'Calm' app's masterclass 'Creative Living Beyond Fear'. 'What's the alternative of trying to do something, trying to make something new? The alternative is to do nothing. And have your tomorrow look exactly the same as today.' Yikes!

She says: 'You do not need a permission slip from the Principal's Office to live a creative life.' And this applies to all of us, especially us parents and carers and those in particular who don't know how to play or voice their needs.

But what if, deep down, you still feel that you do need permission? Well, you actually write that goddamn slip yourself.

PAUSE AND REFLECT

Below, or on a separate piece of paper, create a letterhead.

The Principal's Office

Of [insert your name]

Dear [insert your name]

I am the Principal and this is your permission slip.

You have permission to: (Make your list. Make it broad and wide and funny).

. . . .

. . . .

. . . .

. . . .

. . . .

. . . .

. . . .

. . . .

And you can write more than one permission slip, you know. Over the years I've given myself permission to not aspire to being a perfect parent, to fail at writing my novel, to not write Christmas cards, to stay home and keep life small for a bit, to give myself time to exercise and look after my body each day, to not exercise if I don't feel like it, to do what's best for my kids regarding schooling and follow my instincts.

But for now, we're thinking about fun and play and meeting your needs so start there and then add whatever you'd like after that!

Chaos

If, like me, you live with people whose executive skills are lagging, which means that their ability to organize their belongings is limited and their aptitude to lose their crucial stuff is expansive, then you might, also like me, live in chaos, tinged with dirt. You might also fall into this category yourself.

Some or all of you in your home probably enjoy clean and tidy spaces. It helps rinse your mind and senses, and yet here you are unable to achieve it, even for your sanity. The task is too overwhelming or impossible to maintain because stuff comes out of the kids' rooms like an avalanche the minute you've placed it back up there.

One friend of mine described her family as a benign group of soldier ants who were stoically and methodically emptying the contents of their rooms into the shared living space as if their lives depended on it. I love this description because it represents the fresh-faced enthusiasm of those I love spreading their stuff as they go and 'disapparating' out of clothes in the bathroom and hallway without thought of what then happens to those said items. AND in all fairness, though I do have strong executive skills, over time my survival strategy has become to put away less of my own belongings and to care less. Acceptance and all that!

But there comes a day when the mess gets everyone down. It creates chaos in the mind and body. Here is how I've learned to tackle it.

I keep one room clean. If that's too much, just pick a side of a room! For me, usually it's my front room as I've decluttered that one and so it's easier to do a quick tidy. I've also painted the walls and ceiling a dark, inky blue so it feels like my favourite café and a cocoon. In Café Cocoon I can invite a friend round for coffee and be supervizing my children whilst also having some space. My approach to housework over the years had become to just not invite anyone over, ever. Then I didn't need to feel bad about it. But the front room has been a game changer for me.

I've also recently discovered that the front door area and hallway are minimum effort for maximum benefit. A cheerfully painted front door and clear hallway and stairs make me feel like the house is pleasant when, in reality, if you open any door the detritus will probably flood out like an incoming tide.

Occasionally, I also declutter and tidy my own room as this is the least likely to get messed up so quickly, so it's worth the effort. Plus, it's nicer to sleep in when it's tidy.

Now, I've spent years listening to other parents who get their kids to pick up their toys (trained from birth no doubt) and tidy their rooms once a week. These aren't my kids. Mine struggle to know where to start, how to organize, to make all those nano-decisions of where to put things and what to throw out, and usually the task feels so big and overwhelming that they can't begin even when they want to.

So mostly, I accept the mess, but when I see or hear that it's getting to them, I offer my support. It's a really good time to connect if your productivity expectations are low.

If it helps, put on some music of your child's choosing to move things along and encourage the brain to focus. Then give them one small task that has only one step to it. 'Can you put this pile of Lego® into this box?', 'Can you take the pillowcase off this pillow?' or 'Can you put these folded clothes into that drawer?' Whilst they get on with that, you too pick a task and tackle it. You'll probably be doing five tasks to their one.

You might also be having to keep up a conversation about one of their points of interest.

But when you can, explain out loud that when a job feels too big you just start with one small thing. Then another. These feel manageable and often are a way in because before you know it a lot has been achieved. I do this with the dishwasher. I groan when I find it full and clean but tell myself that whilst I'm boiling the kettle, I'll just put the cups away. After that, I'll just finish that top drawer. Then maybe just the cutlery. Now I'm almost there, I'll just do the saucepans and then, oh, it's almost done, might as well complete what's left of the bottom drawer. Weirdly, there's this part of my brain that knows exactly what I'm up to when I say 'just the cups whilst the kettle is boiling' and yet it's happy to play along!

Usually, in the room-cleaning scenario, an old toy or diary or something of interest is rediscovered which then piques their interest for the next 40 minutes whilst you do most of the tidying. But when all is said and done, you've role-modelled, you've connected and you'll have cleared a bit of space if not all, and they will be super-happy as now they can play in that space (and mess it up instantly) whilst you have a cup of coffee.

Collectors

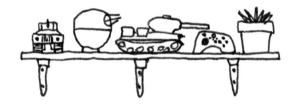

This brings me on to any collectors you have in the family. Not all neurodiverse children collect stuff, but many do have obsessions, and these obsessions often culminate in rather remarkable collections in my experience!

Unless you are happy for your kids to sail off into a future of becoming a hoarder, it's good early on to explain that space in a house is finite. Less space and crammed rooms are not pleasant to live in and affect your mental health.

It may be that an old collection can be kept for memories or for their own children, but this shouldn't mean everything they've ever owned is put in storage. I encourage my collector to sell old, abandoned collections or parts of them to fund the new, shiny collection that he is currently building.

I help with the advertizing and sales to avoid sentimentality getting in the way of letting go (once I've had his consent of course).

When you gain an item, you lose space. Charity shops and car boot sales can mean cheap and thoughtless purchases to boost serotonin levels that end up becoming boxes of clutter that can't be parted with. It's like caffeine. You're worse off later. I'm so much more thoughtful now about everything we are bringing into the house, everything we are ordering. Not only is it bad for the environment, but it's bad for our environment.

A one-in/one-out scheme is good for those who love clothes, teddies or books.

You may have to break down the process of letting go. Neurodiversity can mean that it's difficult to make decisions in fear of making the wrong one. Adults and kids remain frozen rather than in flow.

Pick a relaxed expanse of time, like a day in the summer holidays. Make tea and snacks. Then start small with a tub of old felt pens or one desk drawer, making sure it's clutter that they are not overly attached to. (Yes, I know they're attached to all of it. But aim for marginally less attached.) In the case of the pens, which ones work and don't work? Create two piles. Which stationery items do you no longer like? This forms a third pile – the giveaway pile. The important part of this process is to get rid of the reject piles as soon as possible. Like the same hour of the same day!

Then focus and comment on how lovely the clear space is afterwards and what a gift they've given themselves in creating this space for other things. Anything that couldn't be decided on can be boxed or bagged in a fourth pile to keep things moving. This gets put away and if they haven't missed these items after a few months it may be easier to let them go. Selling items for pocket money can appeal to some children but be impossible for others. See what works in your family.

Let go of any expectations that these mini-lessons in organizing will come to fruition any time soon. Perhaps look at them as lessons they can draw on when they're older and have built up some stamina to work around their brain types. In the meantime, keep things light and connected, knowing that helping them to tidy their space may make for a calm bedtime or two or a lovely play area/hobby space for a few hours.

Dipping In and Out

Having a neurodiverse child (whether they are diagnosed or not) raises a lot of paperwork, emails, phone calls and appointments if you decide you want financial or educational support. The administration and all the invisible time spent working out what you will say, or nervously anticipating a face-to-face meeting or phone call, takes its toll. It's an additional layer of stress on top of what is already a challenging situation.

At first, I noticed that every time school rang it sparked a flood of adrenaline that lasted for hours. Then school rang so much that I began to feel flooded whenever the phone rang at all. I'm not a person that likes confrontation or feels comfortable with it. My upbringing had taught me to be submissive and co-operative, and yet here I was, on the regular, having to disagree with teachers, headteachers and other professionals in order to advocate for Wilf.

At some point over the years, I began a short course in meditation. It encouraged me to notice what was going on in my body and not try to change it. Just accept what was there.

I tried this out with the knot of anxiety in my chest when dealing with school. I noticed it and rubbed my chest. I felt it there and later I felt it go. After that, whenever I felt the knot, I spoke kindly to myself. 'There it is. The stress. But it comes and it goes. It will go soon. Life's such a rollercoaster.' And I began to see that a bad morning could be followed by a brilliant afternoon, or an amazing day could be followed by a very shitty one. If things were bad, they would soon flip to good again. Life was up and down, and somehow when it was down this was very reassuring. I only had to be kind to myself and wait it out.

A helpful pattern that I got into with the crazy levels of administration was to not be immediately responding all the time to stuff. When things need attending to, I will ring/email all the necessary parties in one sitting. People take days and weeks to reply. I read the replies when I feel in the right mood, not when they arrive, and then I leave any chasing up. I let things go whilst I attend to other areas of my life. I couldn't do this when it was all new, but it's how I operate now, and having spoken to other parents and carers, it's a good strategy for the overwhelmed. After some time has passed and when it feels pressing again, I do a spate of chasing up and moving things on to the next level. I think of this as dipping in and out, imagining a bird gliding on the thermals over a lake, dipping down, beak in the water to catch a fish and then swooping back out into the peaceful wide expanse of sky.

SOMETHING PRACTICAL TO TRY...
Where do you feel the stress in your body?
Notice: is it in the chest or stomach, a tight jaw, behind the eyes, in the head or somewhere else? Everyone has a different physical experience.

Print out a body outline and colour it in to depict how you feel in this moment.
My son and I printed out a ton of these and did them regularly at one point. It's a great way to get you to tune in to what's there and also for children who may be dysregulated and unaware of their emotions to colour what they feel.

Get curious: how does it impact on the next activity and in your day?
Allow the feelings, tensions and emotions to be there.

Find a soft landing place and try out some end-the-stress-cycle activities.

PART THREE

The nitty gritty of how to find your child beneath their behaviours

...and make life easier within your neurodiverse household

Dysregulation

Dysregulation is something that took me years to under-stand. We started with an occupational therapy appointment when my son was in the first few years of primary school. He was finding it hard to sit on the carpet and listen or sit at the table and do work. Two occupational therapists led a fun one-off session where they observed his energy, emotions and movements when doing different things. Some things, such as (and it's different for everyone) adding weight in the form of a weighted blanket, were calming and lowered his arousal level. Other activities, such as bouncing on a giant yoga ball, made his brain go too fast and his limbs and body fly everywhere. (There are great ways to use a yoga ball that are helpful, but left unattended to bounce, without your feet on the floor can be counter-productive in our experience. I've had to get rid of our yoga ball. It caused more problems than it solved, and I came to fear its very existence in the house.)

After this, I learned from a friend who works in this area all about sensory processing. It took many conversations, a book and lots of googling to get my brain around it. I'm not surprised that most teachers don't quite get it or understand that the things that worked for one child are useless with another child, or with the same one on a different day!

Sensory processing goes hand in hand with a wide variety of conditions, including dyslexia, ADHD and autism. But the simple truth is that we are all processing information from our senses all the time. It's only when this information gets in the way of what we're doing or need to do that it causes us a problem. Or if our unconscious attempts to balance ourselves with sensory-seeking behaviours get in the way of doing those things.

It's like this. Some of our senses have the volume turned up and want less information and some are turned down and seek out a stronger input for the brain to feel organized. For example, I am quite sensitive to noise and touch. A tap feels like a slap, and the wrong music or a shout too close to my face can feel like an assault on my brain.

The senses we're talking about include all the usual suspects (sight, taste, touch, hearing and smell) as well as another three you might not be so familiar with: vestibular (balance and body position), proprioceptive (movement of muscles, tendons and the like and the detection of external pressure) and interoceptive (what's happening inside our bodies such as hunger, nausea, etc.).

Your child may have sensory-processing issues, which is where they don't instinctively balance themselves to cope with what's going on. They might not recognize that they are thirsty and get a glass of water, or hot, so don't take their jumper off. Both of these issues and a million more may affect their mood and ability to complete tasks/think straight. And their typical sensory preferences might also change depending on what is going on around them and in their bodies.

They might have sensory-processing disorder, which is when the issues are experienced so intensely, that it's impossible to get simple tasks done without a meltdown or a shutdown. For example, many children are so sensitive to touch that brushing hair or teeth is a traumatic battle. Some can't bear the feel of clothes and want to walk around naked, long past the age when that's acceptable if the elderly neighbour pops over.

Over a period of time, observing and questioning with curiosity, you'll get to know what slows your kid down and what speeds them up, what balances them and derails them, and you'll also work out what makes the rest of you tick in the family too.

Professionals may suggest introducing a sensory-enriched diet/environment. This felt to me like a massive and overwhelming chore when we had so much else going on. Wilf went to three schools – a regular state primary and two specialist ones – and none of them helped much with this. They loved to hand out a squishy or a poppet, but despite all the lovely, detailed information I shared, didn't ever help Wilf with efficient sensory breaks. Probably because it would be a full-time job.

When you really know your child well, you'll see that making noises, climbing, wrestling games, chewing sleeves, raiding the fridge, running off, repetitive words, loud music, etc. are all their attempts to balance themselves. And yet, unfairly, these are often the things they get into trouble for doing.

Under all the diagnoses your child may or may not have, any attachment issues and the sensory processing is this thing called dysregulation. It took me years to fully understand that you could spend your whole day, and I often did, dealing with the sensory stuff and all the other things, but the core thing at the bottom of it all is the dysregulation: not being able to regulate your body's needs and emotions, which shows up as behaviour, and in conditions like ADHD and autism body regulation is a lagging skill.

The extremely good news is that this skill can in time be built up to a better point, and talking about it with your child, getting curious and naming what is happening and how you're trying to solve it helps them learn. For us, the most useful thing has been to have constant dialogue about this.

We called the low-arousal state when Wilf is lolling about on the floor or sofa and can't get going 'feeling blue' as we were once shown an arousal 'speedometer' that illustrated this beautifully. Green was a focused, balanced state in the middle and yellow was when the brain and body were running too fast.

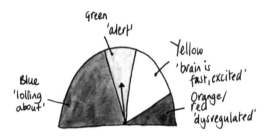

I'm mindful when talking about yellow. My child's superpowers are the fun and enthusiastic side that comes from this yellowy place. So we talked about how yellow can be great at the right time and in the right place. Sometimes you want to be yellow and can enjoy it, but at other times when you want to focus in on something, yellow is too fast to get the job done. Beyond yellow was red. That end of the speedometer represented when things felt so out of balance that they resulted in a meltdown or shutdown.

If your child is difficult to get going in the morning (in the blue zone), then gradual stimulation can be a way forward. Open the curtains and turn any white noise off. Ask them to wiggle their fingers and toes and take their weighted blanket off if they use one. Maybe you could offer some music they like in the background and make gentle conversation whilst you busy yourself in their room. In the evenings, the reverse has to happen.

There are a lot of books and websites with ideas for sensory activities (I'll list some at the end of this chapter) and it's a case of trial and error – helping them to know what they need at different times of the day.

When Wilf reached the teenage years, he no longer felt it was acceptable for me to swish open the curtains early in the morning alongside a flow of cheery chat. All efforts to help him come back to life were sworn at. Since then, we have had to work more collaboratively with Wilf, trying out his ideas and offering but never enforcing solutions. Now he's not in school, it is easier to follow his natural strategies more, and this has led to less stress on both sides, although I must admit mornings are still tricky for him. He thinks certain genres of music help, such as techno. Complications occur when one child requires one set of conditions and the other child the opposite. It's almost impossible for us to all share a family room in a hotel for this reason!

During the day, children seeking more body-to-brain feed-back can benefit from hanging off monkey bars (or an exercise bar in a doorframe works well at home) or swinging in a hammock. (We have inside and outside hammocks even in our tiny house! They can easily be unhooked when not in use.) Ice-cold smoothies sucked through a straw are always met with approval, frozen fruit in a bowl, fizzy water, chewing gum, a chewy, crusty bread roll, crunchy raw veg, salty foods, headphones for music to be played right into the ear and a weighted blanket have all been great hits for us. But of course, your child may need the exact opposite or something completely different.

Over time, explore your own sensory and dysregulation issues. We all have them, and it's useful for your child to see and hear that we all become dysregulated. Give a running commentary on how you're resolving it. So often, parents leave the room to emotionally regulate, to cry or take a breath and the child is left with the sense that the adult is not quite alright (or the child may be oblivious to it), and then they experience the adult just returning some time later, back to normal.

To help you do this you could print off one of the sensory-processing questionnaires available online. But don't get bogged down in them. Don't even do them if you don't feel like it and are not a person who likes form-filling. This book is about making life easier not harder!

But if you don't mind a form, fill one in for yourself, pass one to your partner and then fill one in for each child asking them about how they experience things. Chat about the differences between you all. It's especially good for children with sensory issues to understand that we all have sensory needs and preferences. The only difference is that some of us instinctively attend to those needs without thinking about it, and others take a while to notice and must then make a conscious decision to help themselves get more comfortable.

The main takeaway for me was to notice what my children naturally do to regulate themselves. Chances are they instinctively do stuff that ticks their box and lowers their stress levels, but just isn't as socially acceptable as we or the school would like. Could you learn to embrace some of them? If you want to suggest a swap, what could you offer instead?

PAUSE AND REFLECT

Start by making a list of all the things your child does to regulate, watching them over a few days and writing it down. Investigate what they are giving themselves or blocking out from their experience. Do they appear to be over-reactive or under-reactive to information from the senses? Do they seek more or less from each system? It's often a combination. More from one and less from another.

Example list:

- biting jumper or toys, chewing paper

- taking off socks and shoes

- rocking

- hanging off things

- climbing

- screeching or banging the table

- fiddling with pen/Blu Tack/paperclip/fiddle toy

- joggling their knee

- covering ears

- spinning

- leaving lessons or running off

- rolling around on the floor

- gagging in response to food.

....
....
....
....
....
....
....

Really consider what could be the function behind each act. It is never a desire to be naughty or disruptive.

And here's where it gets a teeny bit tricky. You might think that a child who bites her jumper needs more movement or pressure in that moment, that she's seeking information using her mouth and teeth. But it's never that clear-cut. That child could be in their nervous system responses (fight, flight, etc.) or be anxiously feeling disconnected. They could even be having too much sensory input and trying to cope with it that way. Our brains are complex. There are things on the list above too that could be caused by postural difficulties or motor-skills co-ordination problems or a lack of sensory discrimination.

And sometimes our children crave something that doesn't actually help to balance them. For example, Wilf used to beg us to tickle him. And what I discovered from my occupational therapist friend is that you should definitely avoid tickling a child, even one that you love who is begging you to. Especially them! Tickling is a mixture of pleasure and pain, and it confuses and disorganizes the brain, something that isn't at all helpful for children with sensory issues.

By doing a bit of detective work, asking for advice from an occupational therapist and reading around the subject you will soon start to build a picture of which actions help and which don't.

For the larger part though, there really is far more peace

to be found in letting your child do the things they feel will instinctively balance them. (Once you start paying attention, you'll soon notice the stuff they do that doesn't help.) Acceptance is the key to this and perhaps some explanations for the school and wider family when needed. Where the behaviours impact on others, explain this to your young person, offering thoughtful swaps without punishing. If you aim to make the swap a better, more satisfying experience, then your child will be more likely to let the old strategies fade away.

Useful resources

Websites:
Angie Voss, asensorylife.com
The free resources on sensoryintegrationeducation.com

Books:
Winnie Dunn, *Living Sensationally*
Lucy Miller, *No Longer a Secret* and *Sensational Kids*

Rapport

One day I was driving Wilf to a new specialist school where he had not long started. He had made a friend, but this friend wasn't happy when Wilf didn't want to do something he wanted Wilf to do on a game they were playing online. The new friend had then gone round the school setting everyone against Wilf. Wilf knew he hadn't done anything wrong, but it was stressful and embarrassing that others thought he had.

When we arrived at the school carpark, he refused to get out of the car. I didn't blame him. I knew he didn't feel emotionally supported or safe right in that moment. We sat there for a long time, me trying to lightly cajole him in where I believed support could be found and offering to come in with him. He wouldn't budge. There were staff in the carpark seeing in children from all the various taxis that came from far and wide, but they didn't seem to see my plight for a good 15 minutes. Wilf's stress response (freeze) was escalating.

Eventually a man wandered over. Great, I thought. I'm not really in a position to give Wilf the confidence he needs right now seeing as I'm not going to be there with him all day, but this man is. He opened Wilf's passenger door and began to talk to him. But what came next was sadly useless.

'Morning Wilf. You alright?'
'No.'
'Time to come in now.'
'I don't want to.'
'You've got to come in. Everyone has to go to school... er... you're causing a problem for your mum here, Wilf. Come on, she needs to get on with her day and you're holding her up.'

I couldn't quite believe my ears. A heady mix of emotional manipulation and shaming. After a painful five minutes of this, where I was a little too taken aback to respond, I got to the point that I was actually glad Wilf wasn't going with this man. I knew he had no ability to bolster Wilf and hold the situation emotionally and so did Wilf.

Eventually the man stopped trying and alerted another colleague. A second man came to Wilf's door.

'Wilf!' He greeted him like they were old buddies (even though he'd only met him a couple of times) and in a way that conveyed he was happy to see him. I felt Wilf relax a tiny bit next to me.

'Alright, mate? I'm so glad you're here. I've got something awesome to show you and I think you're about the only one who's going to fully appreciate it.' It was a computer app that he had set up to make some Lego® stop-motion animations. The man's tone of voice was breezy. His interactions lacked tension or force or expectation. He instantly made Wilf feel seen and liked and got in rapport with him. Wilf sprang out of the car with a 'See you later.'

As I drove home, I replayed what had happened before my very eyes. Something that happens a billion times a day in that school and schools and households everywhere I bet. Everyone knows communication is key. It's so well documented that it's boring to discuss, but with neurodiverse kids who feel unheld, misunderstood, disliked and generally low in self-esteem, each moment in a tense environment like that is fragile.

I sometimes think that rapport is one of the things at the bottom of it all. Yes, I know I already said dysregulation was at the bottom. Admittedly there's a lot of things down there. The list gets longer every day. But rapport is so overlooked and yet massively important.

Connection is going to be the closest thing you have to finding the thing that turns any of it around. This is your home base and the area you most need to place your time and attention.

Easier said than done, I know. Neurodiverse folk can so often find connecting with others hard. It's another of those lagging skills. In family gatherings, for example, they may be disconnected, bobbling about on their own until the next person with rapport-building skills shows up.

I've also witnessed apparent conversations where two neurodiverse children are talking and neither is particularly listening or responding to what the other one is saying; they're just carrying on when it's their turn to impart information about their subject of interest!

I asked my son who he felt connected to in his life – I listed various friends and people on both sides of our family. He's a chatty, jolly kid but the list was short: me, his dad, his sister (sometimes) and my mum. He genuinely loved all the others, but he didn't feel properly connected to them.

It's important to take regular opportunities to connect with your child on good days. You can, where they are willing, invite them into your interests and run with that, but it's also important wherever you can to immerse yourself in their hobbies or at least dip in.

I've embraced fossil hunting and dinosaurs, whilst my husband Steve follows all the *Star Wars* spin-off episodes and *Jurassic Park*. We both know more than we'd ever wish to about *Clone Wars* Lego® sets, *Minecraft*, WW2 and looking after a bearded dragon. Steve got Wilf into surfing. I got him into being read to which led to audio books. Other fads come and go. *Pokémon* raised its head more times than I'd like to remember.

Whenever Wilf is stressed, one of the things that sometimes works is to chat to him in a calm tone of voice about his hobbies. Maybe not straight away, but when you see an opening. I'll ask him what videos he was just watching and, based on that, I'll go on to ask what did so-and-so YouTuber say today? What game was he reviewing? Did he think it was any good? I'll ask a question and let him run. Then I'll actively listen to what he's saying and ask another question based on that. Very soon we have built a temporary bridge of rapport. Sometimes this bridge allows us to just get on with the next thing we need to do, and the conversation sails us right through. Rapport helps with transition moments in the day, being out and about, minor frustrations, overwhelm, stressful situations like queuing, waiting for appointments, trying out new things and when things go wrong. Wilf has come to understand what I'm doing, but he still enters into it. It's like a held-out hand that he takes when we both need to be on the same page.

I spent hours trying to explain this at school. I'd heard the term somewhere – 'connection before correction' – and it made a lot of sense to me although the word *correction* sounds very harsh. I prefer 'connection before collection' (as in before you collect them up in whatever activity you're trying to engage them in and take them along with you) or 'connection before re-direction' (where you guide the focus to somewhere more useful).

When things go wrong, I usually start with an acknowledgement of feelings. 'How are you right now?' The answer will probably be a swear word or that they are stressed. Reflect that back. 'Yeah, I can see that was stressful for you.' Even if you feel they are in the wrong, it's still truthful to acknowledge their stress response and how hard that moment was for them. 'Let's go and make a cup of tea? Would you like to walk around the block? What would help right now? Would you like to have a shower/listen to music/go to the sensory room (if at school)/get a snack?'

Usually, Wilf wants to do something that escapes the situation. In my experience, walking away to another area if in school or going on his phone/taking a shower if at home can reset the moment. Don't worry about the phone, you can still use this in your rapport building. 'Sure, take ten minutes to chill out on your phone, good idea. Shall I make us both a drink?' Transitioning off the phone can be hard, but less hard than a meltdown. Pick your hard.

A bit later, you get in rapport off-topic (or rather away from the current situation and onto a topic they are enthused over): 'So, what are you watching/playing?' and 'Oh great, is it going well? What have you managed to complete/draw/ build/trade, etc.?'

After you are back in rapport, you pop/plunge back onto the difficult situation and listen to their viewpoint about what happened (this might be ten minutes later or two hours later or the next day – you need to use your instincts and not rush this part), and gently and kindly explain other people's viewpoints, how you or others have been impacted; then back into rapport and on into the rest of the day. Talking about it might make your child upset or angry again. Pick out the most important thing you want to know or want to say. Keep it short and then go back into a calming activity followed by more rapport building.

You don't get anywhere without rapport, and you can't rush it. Don't even try. If your child does not reply or engage with the chat about their game or hobby, try another topic. What was the last thing they were excitedly talking about? Think back. It might be something less obvious than a hobby, such as putting together an outfit, a TV series they are binge watching, music, a book they're reading. It might be something so far from your understanding that you don't know where to start – some manga fantasy world you know nothing about. Ask what they like about it. Who's their favourite character and why? Ask to watch YouTube snippets.

If there is still no engagement stop and try again later.

The key to rapport is a funny one. I once spent a year learning NLP (neuro-linguistic programming), which is all about communication under the microscope, the language patterns we use, our tone of voice and body language. To save you the time and money, this is what I learned in a nutshell.

In a 1981 study a body language expert, called Albert Mehrabian, found that effective communication is broken down into:

- words – 7%

- body language – 55%

- tone of voice – 38%.

Look how important body language is. And a whopping 93% of communication is nonverbal. Only 7% words. So, it doesn't matter how reasonable you are being in your conversation, if you have even a whiff of authority or judgement or anger in your tone, your child is going to react to that. And this is even more apparent in children with ADHD, autism and PDA (pathological demand avoidance).

If you can tell that your emotions or stress levels are running high, take a moment to centre yourself. It can be really beneficial to explain that you need time to regulate and that you're going to walk to the other side of the room or beyond and take some breaths. (The reason for this is you don't want them to feel rejected and insecure by you walking away – it just makes matters worse. So be literal and know that you are role-modelling.)

If it is safe to leave the room, do so and calm down. Take those breaths, ground yourself, make a hot drink if it helps, or try one of the things from your previously created self-care list and then return. Feel free to explain what you've done to balance yourself.

Consider your body language and tone of voice. If you're not sure, think about people you know who are easy-breezy. Perhaps there is a teacher or teaching assistant at school who is just so casual in their approach, nothing is a problem. Or midwives, I've noticed, have this cheery, chatty air too. Probably because in some cases they meet a woman and then have to inspect her parts and sometimes shove a gloved hand up there to see what's going on, all within a very short space of time! They need to build instant rapport like a mother****er when you think about it. They're the kings and queens of rapport. Nurses too. Or maybe a friend or colleague has it? Whoever comes to mind, hold them in your head and act as if you're them or a you-shaped version of them.

Next time there's an upset, throw in a hint of them and see what happens. This casual demeanour is one that you build like a muscle and learn to snap into over time. It might be rubbish to start with... keep going. Notice when you see it in others, or on television. It's a lifetime's acting role, and you're doing the method-acting approach where you live it for years in advance of the movie being made. It's not fake though. There is an easy-breezy side to all of us if we look for it. Dredge that mamma/daddy up and bring them into play.

PAUSE AND REFLECT

Who do you know who has a light and casual, warm approach? It could be your partner, a person you know well or only a little, a celebrity or even a character from a book or film. Notice how they behave and note it down here...

. . . .

. . . .

. . . .

. . . .

Break it down.
What is their tone of voice like?

. . . .

. . . .

. . . .

. . . .

What sort of body language do they have?

. . . .

. . . .

. . . .

. . . .

Are they fast or slow to move?

. . . .

. . . .

. . . .

. . . .

What does their energy feel like?

. . . .

. . . .

. . . .

. . . .

Do they laugh a lot or get down on a level to meet your child? Do they act like nothing's a problem? How do they show interest in what you or others are saying or doing?

. . . .

. . . .

. . . .

. . . .

SOMETHING PRACTICAL TO TRY...

Sometimes actors use costume to get into a role. I'm not suggesting you dress up whenever you want to build rapport. That would be cra-zy! But an interesting idea to help cement this new role you are establishing would be to choose an inconspicuous reminder of what you're trying to achieve. A friendship bracelet, leather band or necklace with a meaningful charm attached could be something you touch each time to consciously remind yourself of the need to build rapport. You could add the mantra 'Connection before collection' too or something similar. If you touch this each time you consciously attempt to build rapport, it will become an anchor point, which will over time ping you into the helpful internal response, that easy-breezy, see the humour in it all and the child beneath the behaviours person, the bridge that you're aiming for. If you think this might be helpful, you can learn more about NLP anchors on YouTube.

What could you make, find in your belongings or buy to form an anchor?

Tick this box when you have it on!
☐

Declarative Language Is Not Just for PDAers

So many times I read a self-help book or do a course and I'm full of good intentions. But the day-to-day reality of noticing when I need to implement my new knowledge and then smoothly bring it out to make a difference turns out to be nigh on impossible.

I felt this very strongly when I studied NLP (neuro-linguistic programming) for a year. NLP requires you to notice what you are saying and how you are saying it, to word things differently, challenge your beliefs and reframe ideas. There's a lot to be aware of and remember. I know, in theory, that if I politely request my teenager to empty their room of dirty crockery and my tone of voice displays all my annoyance, I'm more likely to become the wall they want to push back off. But knowing this, incredibly, does not seem to stop me doing it.

Considering your tone of voice, body language and sentence structure is a muscle that requires building up. And perhaps for most people it's not worth the effort.

However, for parents of kids with pathological demand avoidance (PDA) it perhaps is worth the effort. It's maybe the difference between coping and crisis. Maybe. PDA is still not fully understood; it can exist on its own, alongside autism or alongside ADHD, and the core reasons for the behaviour can be very different from one person to another.

What it can look like is someone who always wants to be in control, gets highly agitated and anxious or shuts down when out of control, says no, doesn't do the things they're being asked to do and can't stand being asked to do anything directly or implicitly. Any whiff of a request or expectation overloads their system. Even when it is coming from within them and in line with what they want to do.

Like most of these things, there are good and bad days. On a day where a child has been masking in school (holding all their behaviours in to fit the system and culture) their capacity for demands is going to be a lot lower.

The reasons for these behaviours are extremely varied. The person reacting to the request to do something may dislike the change, uncertainty and unpredictability involved. The demand or expectation may bring an actual or anticipated sensory overload in either its social aspect or environmental aspect. It may have associations with or bring back distressing memories of past experiences that were unpleasant. In a situation where an adult is trying to convince a child to do something, the weight of how much they want the thing done may be apparent in their attitude, words, tone or body language, and this weight of expectation could tip the young person into a PDA response. It could be that the child is focused on something they are absorbed in and don't want to make a transition away from it. It could be that they perceive the task to be boring (the idea of which literally hurts some brains) or too challenging, or that it may result in getting things wrong, which could lead to being told off and feeling bad about themselves. Lagging executive function could make the task feel huge and unstartable.

Those make sense when you understand autism and ADHD, but PDA on its own can also be set off by literally just the expectation of others causing stress and anxiety – other people's needs or plans can be very triggering for those brain types, where a demand is felt like an attack or an attempt to control.

It's no surprise that children with PDA or PDA tendencies find the education system hard. It's literally full to the brim with demands and expectations to follow authority. Teachers have that 'obey me' tone of voice that they employ. A time-table is literally a whole page of expectations, homework is a list of demands, etc. And there's no room for autonomy.

And yet we need all brains for the development of civilization. And neurodiverse brains in all their richness are nearly always the ones moving along thoughts and actions within our workplaces and communities because they don't just follow directives. They think for themselves. So an education system that doesn't meet them is a flawed one.

When a child is distressed (whether that's visible or not), oppositional behaviour is self-preserving, and as a parent, when you understand the reasons behind it, whether those behaviours are consciously made or compulsive and part of the person's survival instincts, you can approach the situation from a different angle.

Parents learning to work around PDA are advized to take a low-demand approach. Declarative language, in particular, is talked about in conjunction with PDA kids, but I have come to understand it's a game changer with all neurodiverse kids and all teenagers whatever their brain types.

When you think about it, anxiety, lagging executive skills, inaction, slower processing times and oppositional moments are constantly being met with our directives, cajoling, instructions, criticisms, nagging and need for control.

Over time this kind of shapes your interactions with your

children... and can even lead a parent to think their child has PDA when they don't. (And who the hell really knows? PDA was once thought to be an absolute and is now considered to have a spectrum.)

What we do know is that when two neurotypical people are relating, their interactions tend to be 80% declarative language (statements and observations) and 20% imperative language (anything that requires a response). They spend more time sharing thoughts, feelings and perspectives, than questioning, prompting and directing.

On the other hand, when neurotypicals are conversing with neurodiverse people, it tends to be the opposite. If the neurodiverse person struggles with getting the right words out, the neurotypical person will jump in and try and maintain the interaction by asking more questions to draw a response, and it often ends up about 80% imperative and 20% declarative, making them more anxious. Instead of making it easier to relate, it's unwittingly making it harder.

So, what really is declarative language? It's basically a form of commentary, where you share information in a relaxed and open way. Instead of telling your kids what to do, instructing them or asking them questions that expect a response, which can result in them becoming oppositional or shutting down, you thoughtfully give them the information to make important discoveries in the moment.

Imperative: 'Put your shoes on.'

Declarative: 'I've got my shoes on and am ready to go.'

Wait ten seconds to allow for processing time. Then if nothing has happened try a second declarative statement. Then ten seconds or more. Then a third. It's crucial not to revert to a question or instruction.

Declarative statements include: sharing your thoughts, feelings and ideas about something; describing events; sharing experiences and knowledge; and any other interaction that is non-demanding. It doesn't ask anything of the listener and therefore does not produce performance anxiety.

A simplified example would be, 'I fancy cheese today in my sandwich.' It does not require a response but may lead the listener into sharing, 'I also like/want cheese' or 'I don't like/want it' or 'I'd like ham and finely sliced gherkins'. They may not share anything and that needs to be ok. You are not tricking them into disclosing their sandwich-filling requests. You are taking away the demand.

It is also key to use a declarative approach. Instead of being the messenger (delivering the demand) and getting shot at (as the demand has caused your child to dysregulate), try to stand beside the demand. Be honest about where a demand comes from and how you feel about it. For example:

You: 'The doctor has suggested that if you use this cream, it will soothe that sore patch of skin.'

The young person: 'No, not gonna happen.'

You: 'It's a tricky one isn't it, because I'm hearing that you're in a lot of discomfort and the cream might make that go away quicker, but I can also see that you are not keen and I'm not going to make you use it. It's entirely up to you. I'll leave it downstairs.'

(Later) The young person: 'Mum, it hurts so much.'

You: 'Aww I'm so sorry to hear that. The body takes time to heal itself. It might take a couple of weeks, but it will get there eventually. Bodies are amazing like that. You know where the cream is though, if you'd like to speed things up.'

I'm not saying this dialogue will solve everybody's medicine problems, but battling it out, pinning them down, following them around with it or whatever has failed before was probably too confrontational and resulted in chipping away at your relationship. Lay the demand down. Look at it with them, agree that it's annoying (you'd rather not be spending time thinking about it either), but it's available if they want it and no problem if they don't. Whatever pain made them ask you to procure it in the first place might lead them to giving it a go when they truly feel that all expectation has gone. It might not the first few times, but if you've been struggling, give this approach some time. It's worth a go!

In time, these language choices and sharing opportunities build resilience, flexibility and positive relationships. The lack of nagging also helps. And the reason it takes time is that trust needs to be built.

It's vital to respond to any low-level resistance with backing off. Even if just at first, to allow space and time to process.

And why not explain what you've learned and how you intend to do things differently and then use explicit low-demand sentence starters, such as:

- 'I can't make you...'

- 'I'm not going to force it...'

- 'It's up to you...'

If, for example, you start well with a statement and then, exasperated, follow with a question or demand, your efforts may well lose their value and be mistrusted in the future. Similarly, if you use declarative language to wangle your child into doing something (even if it's something they previously said they wanted to do), this will be sniffed out and mistrusted next time. Trust is built incrementally.

As with any approach, these language patterns should be used carefully and with an ethical intention. They should not be used to emotionally manipulate a child or trick them into doing something the way you want it done or even something they want done.

It's not about disguising a demand either. It is done to provide information that allows them to make their own decisions and choices.

Helpful sentence structures:

- Cognitive verbs such as *I think... I wonder... I remember... I know... I imagine... I wish...*

- Words that emphasize uncertainty and possibility, such as *maybe, possibly, perhaps, sometimes*

- Words that describe your feelings and senses, such as *I smell... I see... I hear... I feel...*

- Using *I* and *we* instead of *you.*

But this book isn't about making your life harder. So where to start? There are books and workshops on this emerging subject for anyone who's had their interest sparked. Workshops where you get to practise declarative language are definitely a great way forward.

For everyone else, now you've got the bigger picture, start by picking one small manageable thing to work on so you don't get overwhelmed.

I don't always get communicating with my kids right. I'm an honest, direct person and can be quite blunt without meaning to be. I can also be tired and exasperated and, ok, controlling and naggy. My children have struggled, feeling out of control, both at home and school, and out of all that I've described, what I've found helpful on difficult days is to uncover the requests and demands and then stand next to them, alongside my child. And to let go of any authority or investment I have in the situation. At first it came from a quietly flabbergasted state, but when I saw how it played out, I adopted it. These are the kids you need to treat as equals. They need to be in control of their own decisions and lifestyles and that might mean getting things wrong so that they can learn for themselves.

The idea is to provide full context and information and then leave space for autonomy. How you would speak to another autonomous adult – we're aiming for that.

PAUSE AND REFLECT

So… is there a small, frequently occurring situation in your household that would usually end in opposition or a shut-down? (I'm thinking teeth cleaning, but that might be a biggy in some families.) Pick something super-small and insignificant to practise on.

What is it? Write it down here.

. . . .

. . . .

. . . .

. . . .

. . . .

. . . .

. . . .

You can even practise on your grumpy, neurotypical teen-ager first – because it's also a great approach to anybody transitioning from parenting a child, to parenting a teenager that's becoming an adult.

I am very new to this path but when I came across it, it inspired me to ask a lot less and state how I feel out loud a lot more, to let go of desired outcomes and only have expectations of myself.

The transformation for me came when I realized that I could state that I'm going for a walk and some fresh air and offer for my child to join me, or I could invite them to hang out together at home, and if they chose not to take that up, that was ok.

I make the time and create the opportunity, which means my side of the parenting is complete. How they choose to respond and what they take me up on is up to them. Using this approach, which runs right through my body (the expectations aren't hidden, they are no longer there), means that my child takes up opportunities more often than when they felt they were being cajoled and manipulated. It's another do-less approach! The key points are:

- Stop trying to tell your child what to do.

- Don't disguise demands.

- Uncover and stand beside expectations and demands.

- Give your child as much autonomy over their everyday life as you can.

PAUSE AND REFLECT

Taking these ideas into consideration how will you now approach the small but regular problem situation you wrote down? Be specific in what you might say and how you might say it.

Getting Curious

I hosed down his wetsuit and hung it out in the last of the September sun. A bee came and whispered in my ear: 'This won't break you. You're stronger than you'll ever know.' That's what I thought I heard anyway, before it hummed away.

I scan the news of Wilf's day. Good outdoor ed visit to the river? Wet wetsuit indicates he went in. Wetsuit shoes no longer with us. Drawings at the bottom of his bag, crumpled and now damp, apparently done in the head's office this afternoon. He was too tired to go to lessons after swimming. Those are the facts of the day. There's not that many yet. I will be able to shade a bit more in as the evening wears on.

How much more can he take? Are we waiting for a crack? Why is it so hard to make that leap and free fall into home education? My mind thinks back to drop-off that morning.

'Don't leave me, Mum,' he says, looking younger than his years. 'Why can't you stay? If you stayed everything would be ok.' It's the same every morning.

My dear boy. His fresh face is troubled. He wants to be able to do school like everyone else, but he can't. Not easily. One telling off and his whole day spirals. Why do they tell him off? Why can't they listen?

What did you do today? I ask at each pickup, trying to sound casual.

'I don't know. I don't know what lessons I had. I don't know who I saw at lunchtime. I don't know.'

Later, in his own words, he says something like: 'Somewhere my brain knows, but it doesn't want to go back there. I don't want to fish back through it all and see the day's flash points. I don't want you to be disappointed that I got it wrong because I need you right now. I'm sorry, Mum, I just can't go back in there and re-live it all for you. It was bad enough the first time.'

On that particular day he was in Year 7 at a small independent school that had a focus on outdoor adventure. It was slipping into special measures, and many of the staff chose to work there because they couldn't cope with mainstream. But it was harder than mainstream. Most of the kids needed 1:1 and none of them had it. Children and adults alike were dysregulated and unaware of their needs. They were trying to keep the structure of a school but with slightly more flexibility. It was never enough.

ALL behaviour is communication. I have said it countless times to teachers and teaching assistants and found very few able to take the time to explore. They are always under enormous time constraints from the job. It's left me wondering what home and classrooms would be like if parents and educators explored all behaviour with patient curiosity. When kids are not emotionally wounded, stressed and dysregulated, they are flipping amazing. All of them.

Our children are not their behaviours. Those are coping strategies. Our children are treasures underneath those behaviours. In a dysregulated household, each day the real child needs to be sort of excavated at regular intervals so that you can re-connect with them at a core level.

When I got curious about Wilf's day, I could see what happened before an incident. Maybe he hadn't eaten lunch, or he'd been stressed about a task. Maybe he'd done a task brilliantly and then another one had appeared and then another one, and he just didn't have the resilience to cope because each task took so much more out of him than it did for the average child. Maybe there was a supply teacher and he or she had used an authoritative tone of voice, or a teaching assistant had threatened to take points away and he'd been in his stress response. If any of these things (or a million more) happened, he would start to say no and become repetitive.

Your child will have the thing they do when things start to be uncomfortable for them and then the things they do when they are fully overloaded and stressed out.

You should not be aiming to fix the behaviours. But instead to get curious around the warning signs and lead your children to notice them too. Self-awareness is going to be useful to them in adult life.

How to get curious

Stage 1
When your child is in the thick of their stress response, they cannot think straight. None of us can. (Our brains release hormones when we're feeling threatened and then use the survival parts, which are limited in their thinking.) This is not the time to get your point across or try and rationalize a situation to them.

If their behaviour meets your stress response, things are just going to escalate. Don't take their behaviour personally, however much they hurl insults and anger. They are reacting to a situation. Stand beside that thing.

Are you able to stay in your core, regulated self or do you

become dysregulated when your child is stressed out? That's the first thing to address. Maybe you're going to need to spend time working on that centre line or using breathwork or experimenting with all the suggestions in the first part of this journal so that, more often than not, you're keeping cool.

Then... validate their feelings: 'I can see this is really hard for you sweetheart' or 'This is a tough one buddy. I can see you're stressed/angry/afraid right now.' You're not validating their behaviour, just their feelings. They need you to believe them. 'I believe you. This feels hard for you right now.' This takes a lot of heat out of the situation. You may actually see their bodies relax a teeny bit.

At this point, questions need to be minimal and given with an attitude of love and kindness. Tone of voice is crucial here. One of the following questions might help:

- 'Where do you need to be right now to feel calm?'

- 'Do you want to go to the sensory room/your bedroom or pull on your weighted blanket?'

- 'Would you like to splash some water on your face [calms the vagus nerve] or drink a glass of water?'

- 'Would you like a walk around the block?'

- 'Do you want to do something together or be left alone?'

Just slowly ask one question, allowing for processing where needed – something my double-quick brain has had to adjust to. Do not ask another question until the one you've just asked has been answered as you will overwhelm your child, who may be slowly mulling the first question over.

Notice what they try out and whether it helps to calm them. Comment on this gently as you go along and do all the things you suggest alongside them. So, you both splash water on your face or use a cool flannel and then you say, 'It's amazing how splashing your face with water helps. It calms the nervous fight or flight system.' Lead them to a soft landing place, but lead them as a team member – you're in this together.

Stage 2

A few hours later or another day it's possible to get more detail. Ask questions, but mostly listen, just querying some details. Get curious about what was underneath the behaviour. It's often a feeling of being out of control or a situation that is unfair or misinterpreted. Schools are very controlling places (and we parents can be too!) and some teachers lean in to this fully.

You may have a nugget of information provided by the school. 'They ran out! They got really angry! They threw a chair! They swore at someone!' It's often true AND a warped perspective at the same time. You can tell your child a small bit of what you heard to home in on what you want to hear more about. Then lightly add a question:

- 'Did something go wrong today?'

- 'Was something unfair?'

- 'Is this true?'

- 'What do you think happened?'

Then you listen with all the body language and expressions of someone that is sympathetic to your child's plight. Some of their actions and coping strategies may have caused mayhem and brought about some negativity from staff, but all this behaviour tells you something, and lots of specific things if you listen. It's packed with info. Remember that anger is nearly always a few steps away from tears. It's an emotion that represents that a boundary has been crossed for that person. Your child's boundaries may well be very different from your own, but they are their boundaries. Explore them.

One of the best places to listen to my child is in the car, just me and him right next to me in the passenger seat. Sometimes, when he was little, I made up a reason to get into the car and just drive about so that Wilf could talk and I could listen. (Stopping off for snacks helps majorly with keeping in rapport.)

Other activities that have you alongside, rather than staring them in the eyeballs, are also good. I've tried board games,

Uno, walking round the block and cycling, all of which were effective on some days and not on others. With cycling you need to be able to get on a track where you can ride next to each other. Other friends say washing up together or cooking can be good. I've not experienced this in my house, but all children are different. If you can link up with them on one of their games, a quiet moment where not much is happening might be a great place, or they may need to be looking at their screens whilst listening. This generation seem to have the ability to be attending to multimedia input all at once, so don't force them to be quiet and look at you and listen. Try out some more casual approaches and listen more than you talk.

Often, at school, Wilf made 'bad choices' as they term it, whilst in his stress responses. I wanted to scream when I heard 'bad choices'. These were never conscious choices – more like stress-based reactions and survival strategies that kept him sane.

If teachers had taken the time to get in rapport with him (connection always first) and then casually suggest they take a walk or get a cup of tea or a crunchy snack together (this sounds far-fetched in a mainstream situation, but is entirely possible in a specialist setting), they might have found out why he'd been angry (afraid/ashamed/frustrated/rejected), and then everyone would know something useful. Our emotions are always information about us for us to learn from.

PAUSE AND REFLECT

When things go wrong how does your child act? Do they walk off, look at their screen, get physical and sometimes destructive? Get curious and write it all down here.

. . . .

. . . .

. . . .

. . . .

. . . .

. . . .

Chances are that they are doing things to calm down, albeit these might not always be socially acceptable things (shutting down, yelling, turning tables over, ruining a display, jumping the school gate and legging it).

Offer your child some re-balancing skills and observe whether any help a little bit. One tick for tried and two ticks for successful, even if only in a small subtle way.

- ☐ Time in a sensory room/tent – you can make a cubby hole anywhere with blankets.

- ☐ Weighted blanket burrito (roll them up in blanket).

- ☐ Splash cool water on face.

- ☐ Drink a glass of water/squash.

- ☐ Change of scene – a walk around the block (take tea for you and snacks if they like picnics).

- ☐ Nature – a walk around the nearest park or green space.

- ☐ Bare feet on the earth.

- ☐ Hanging from monkey bars or doorframe exercise bar.

- ☐ Swinging in hammock or on a swing.

- ☐ Rocking on a rocking chair or just rocking themselves.

- ☐ Crunchy, salty or frozen food.

- ☐ Hitting a punchbag – you can make one out of a stuffed laundry bag hung off a doorframe exercise bar.

- ☐ Ripping up cardboard.

- ☐ Connection with a balanced adult (calm nervous system).

- ☐ Playing a game on their phone for an agreed amount of time. Ten minutes of chess/word game or a basic game, rather than hours of their usual game of choice, may help you allocate extra time if they have limited screen time. Tetris has now been scientifically proven as a brain relaxant. Paint mixing videos and the like are also good.

☐ Throwing a heavy basketball up against a wall and letting it bounce back to them.

PAUSE AND REFLECT

What do you do to calm yourself when angry or frustrated? List as many things as you can think of (If you're not sure, try out some of the above and see what feels good for you):

. . . .

. . . .

. . . .

. . . .

. . . .

. . . .

. . . .

. . . .

. . . .

. . . .

Shining a Light on BIG Feelings

My neurodiverse kids have big feelings. They are hard to soothe. They feel their feelings and it's raw and messy. The feelings go on and on. Crying does not always appear to be cathartic or act like a full stop.

Sometimes there's numbness and a not wanting to feel, there's a sense of fighting the feelings, pushing them away or pushing them down (disassociation), escaping them through screens, food and distractions. But other times there's cries of outrage, and the waves of distress keep coming.

Right from the start, we hush our babies when they cry. It's what has been passed down to us and it's what our instincts tell us to do. We walk around joggling our little bundles, singing softly and reassuring them. We want to end our children's suffering, so we try to calm their expression of it. How often have you said or heard 'Hush now, stop crying' or 'It's going to be alright'? Or, as I once made the mistake of saying during a very long day of it, 'Just imagine a box, a wooden treasure chest stood under an ancient oak tree and place all your worries in there and shut the lid.'

'STOP feeling my feelings?' asked an outraged Wilf. 'Put a lid on them and let them rot in there? Oh, that sounds very healthy. I thought all feelings were for feeling?'

'Er... when you say it like that...' We both burst out laughing. I think I just needed a rest from his feelings that day, but that wasn't particularly helpful for him. Luckily, he is smart and takes no prisoners. I've had to grow up a lot being his mum!

All feelings *are* for feeling. This is true. That is what I had taught him on a Mary Poppins day. People self-medicate with food, alcohol, drugs, sex and distractions to numb the pain of those feelings. I see my kids' teenage friends starting on that journey and I want to tell them all, but I stick to telling my kids and hope they spread the word. And a large number of neurodiverse kids and young adults self-medicate to survive their anxiety, low self-esteem or an inability to emotionally regulate.

This is something that I learned from the likes of Glennon Doyle and Brené Brown. Glennon explains on her *We Can Do Hard Things* podcast that when she became sober from alcohol and drugs, she realized that those things were not the problem in her life. Those things were just really bad coping strategies. When she took the drugs and alcohol out of the equation, what she was left with was all of her terrifyingly big emotions, and that was the real difficulty in her life.

The good news is that there is no complicated therapeutic approach to this. No longwinded process you have to drag your child through. It's simple:

- Name your feelings.

- Help your child name their feelings.

- Make space for them. Don't soothe them away. Be able to witness them.

Wilf has known a fair bit of loss in his short life. By the end of primary school he'd lost: his gran (whom he saw once a week and loved to play Scrabble with) and had to voice-record a goodbye to her as we were abroad – one of the hardest things any of us has had to do; his grandpa, very unexpectedly (whom he saw all the time and was one of the few people he felt fully seen and loved by); his great gran (whom he sat and said goodbye to as she was in the process of dying); two praying mantis pets in succession; and his favourite stuffed penguin toy that was a real comfort to him. That child owned two tiny funeral suits and a pair of black brogues (all from a charity shop haul my mum found).

The grief came and went, often at bedtime, but the loss of the penguin right at the end of this cluster was probably the last straw. Wilf was bereft. Inconsolable.

He's never coped well with losing things. He's loss adverse. I just googled it and it's definitely a thing. He once lost an old black sock in the swimming pool changing room during a school swimming lesson and, despite all manner of reassurance that we didn't need it, was so upset that I had to walk back to the pool at dinner time and look for it. I couldn't find the sock, but in desperation I picked up some other kid's stinking, damp and discarded sock and gingerly walked it home held between two fingers. I showed it to Wilf who was very much relieved, before casually throwing it straight in the bin after he'd gone off to eat a cheese string in front of the telly.

When we lost the penguin, I knew it wasn't going to be easy. I did everything in my power to find that thing: phone calls, emails, reward posters, lost teddy Facebook pages. And I replaced him with an exact replica, but it wasn't the same. I told Wilf that he hadn't really lost Jon-Jon because Jon-Jon was a part of his imagination, he came from his heart and therefore had never left. He'd always be a part of him. Wilf liked this idea and made me repeat it to him when things felt raw again and again.

As a little aside, before we get back to those strong feelings, bedtime without Jon-Jon was miserable. For months. Until I got to the bottom of what that flappy, annoying penguin with the squarky voice did for him. It's a bit of a diversion, but for any parent whose kid has lost their special, comfort thing or who has trouble going to bed on their own, let me explain.

Primary school Wilf was a cuddly kid with lots of soft toys. He also liked discarded things, such as an old windscreen wiper Steve was throwing out. He has an appreciation for the unwanted, the underdog, loving all the misunderstood baddies in films, and like many kids he had a whole heap of stuffed toys. Unlike many kids his included snakes, sting rays, a giant octopus and a huddle of penguins. They all contributed to create a nest of sorts on his high sleeper platform that Steve built. For quite a while, nothing old or new was hitting that Jon-Jon spot. It was excruciating. The 'Jon-Jon still exists in your heart' speech helped, but it wasn't enough.

Quite often Wilf took toys to bed to play with as he fell asleep: soldiers or *Star Wars* figures or Lego®. I started to notice that he was always asking where this one figure was last thing at night. It was Lego® Captain Rex. Lego® Captain Rex was the very expensive jewel in his Lego® empire. His main birthday present a few months before. At first, I thought Captain Rex was for playing with or for treasure as part of the nest, but then one evening it dawned on me when searching the whole house for this tiny man that Captain Rex was needed. I hadn't taken much notice of *Clone Wars*, often on in the background after school, but now I did. Captain Rex was a bit on the gruff side but morally strong, dependable, loyal and a mentor to his men. He was a tactician and fearless in battle and had a good sense of humour. I saw that Wilf, who had begun to go through a terrible time at school, needed all the back-up that Captain Rex provided to feel secure, and yet it wasn't quite enough.

Over a period of a few days, I asked Wilf some pretty direct questions about how Jon-Jon acted and how he had made him feel. We drew a picture and listed it all out. Jon-Jon had been a big huggable source of comfort, but also a mischievous alter ego. He was loud and impulsive and sometimes rude, but he had a big heart too and was a loyal ally.

The Christmas before he'd got lost, I was in the unfortunate position of visiting my dad every day in intensive care. Nearly all of December was spent there and then he died a few days before Christmas. In between visiting times, I was forced to go home and get on, rather numbly, with the business of Christmas. With both children disliking school, Advent and the countdown to the Christmas hols was always a big deal. I'd started on December 1st, before my dad was ill, positioning Jon-Jon, who had a reputation for being cheeky, in funny scenarios for Wilf to find when he got back from school. There was a video of him playing the piano badly for all the other penguins and shouting out Christmas carols, and Wilf would find him surrounded by empty chocolate wrappers – our version of the elf on the shelf antics. Crazily, I'd just get back from the ICU and I'd have to think on my feet to find something he could be doing, winding him up in tinsel or sticky tape, etc. Some days I just didn't get it done. This was a really sad and traumatic time in my life, but when Wilf came home to nothing, he'd accept a short story of what Jon-Jon had done all day in his absence. I improvized and sometimes what came out was lame, but Wilf was easily pleased on this front. He loved it all. So, you see, Jon-Jon was a fully fleshed, loveable rogue.

When we pulled apart everything that Jon-Jon had fulfilled and everything that Captain Rex was now giving, it didn't match up. So, when one day Wilf insisted he needed a huge goose, I knew that he did.

Wilf had a fascination for a particular goose down at the quay. He called him Al Capone. Al Capone was a huge greylag and although he was big and noisy, he was being picked on and shunned by the resident gaggle, who were your typical white geese, and ignored by the other migrated gaggle who were Canadian. Wilf would sit by Al Capone and feed him goose food he'd carefully researched. He'd talk to and appreciate him until Al Capone came to recognize him. Wilf flapped at any white goose who was giving Al a hard time and gradually raised the respect levels of this greylag to the point that Al Capone came to be right in the centre of the flock.

In my mind, geese were noisy honkers and a bit scary with sharp-looking beaks, but Wilf made me see them differently. They were misunderstood. Al Capone had a truly beautiful soul when calm that even I fell in love with. Their noise came from their own insecurities and their protective response for each other. You might be familiar with the term *silly goose*, which dates right back to the 16th century when geese were widely seen as a symbol of stupidity for flapping about so noisily.

Wilf, I think, felt lacking at school. His behaviours meant that he was treated like a noisy, silly goose. He was too loud, too disruptive, too much and always struggling to get all the work done. But it was all behaviour, a defence mechanism. Unconsciously, he related to how geese behaved and were treated. Al Capone was a bit like the goose incarnation of Jon-Jon, so we bought a ridiculously expensive, life-size goose plush toy that pecked me until I got to know him. I made him a scarf though and duly bought him Christmas chocolates because Goose was a godsend. Goose and Captain Rex were a team. Part of my team, on night duty.

Recently, having learned about parts therapy (Internal Family Systems), I can see that Jon-Jon/Goose were a part of Wilf that needed to be appreciated, loved and accepted by him as role-modelled by me. Perhaps his own love of Goose helped him to heal some of the pain school had inflicted. Captain Rex, I think, was a warrior part. A grown-up in his back pocket that was there when I couldn't be, to give him strength. A protective part maybe? I'm sure a trained IFS practitioner would know.

I indulged the night crew for several years, and in early teenagehood they became less and less required, in the room somewhere, but no longer taken on holidays or needed to fall asleep with.

Interestingly, I was stood with a group of my brother's friends recently, men in their thirties, who were talking about *Clone Wars*; I told the story (an abridged one) of Lego® Captain Rex, and all of them went glassy eyed. They all said, without exception, they wished they had a Captain Rex mentor to make them feel that bit safer in the world! I think we all need someone in our back pocket.

PAUSE AND REFLECT

Take a moment to consider: who would you choose for your own back pocket and why? What need would they fulfil?

It can be one person or several. They might be alive and known to you or someone who has died or you don't know that well but just have a sense of. It might be a celebrity or even a fictional character. You can stick a picture of them in your wallet or on your wall to bring their energy into your life on days when you need it.

. . . .

. . . .

. . . .

. . . .

. . . .

. . . .

A few more things to journal on...

Does your child have a toy that they role-play with? Is it like a version of them with the volume turned up? Could it represent a part of them? What attributes does it have? What could it be giving your child that your child needs right now?

....

....

....

....

....

....

Does your child have a toy that they ask for at night or when in distress? What does it represent to them that perhaps they feel they lack or an area they might believe they need bolstering in?

....

....

....

....

....

....

If your child has lost their comfort toy or does not have a good enough one and is clingy at night, can you help identify people, animals, characters or objects that might help them feel safe, loved, understood, seen, etc. when you're not there?

....

....

....

....

....

....

What can you do to help bring your child's toy to life for them? These are great moments to connect with your child over something they love. Ideas include: tea parties with miniature meals; celebrating their birthdays; making beds and houses out of boxes; making scarfs out of bits of fabric; including them in the bedtime story; helping your child to sew them a tiny stocking that fits two chocolates in; and taking photos of them doing cool stuff.

....

....

....

....

. . . .

. . . .

Simple questions you can ask your child about their toy to find out more:

- 'What do you most like about X?'

- 'What is X's personality like? Can you describe them?'

- 'Is there anything you don't like about X?'

- 'Does X make you feel safe? Comforted? Less alone? Or are they just for playing with so you don't get bored?'

Ask if X likes the food, TV shows and things your child likes. Do they share the same preferences? That could be a sign that they relate to the toy rather than use the toy to compensate their feeling of not being able to deal with everything alone (feeling small, insecure, out of control or helpless).

If the toy is lively, with strong preferences or acts out, it may be the child uses the object to explore and soothe parts of themselves. If the toy is a quiet spectator, it may represent something your child feels they need, such as safety and security. Some dogs and other pets can also fall into this category, giving non-judgemental friendship and unconditional love and/or a calm nervous system that can be borrowed from.

But back to that strong feeling of anguish, the insurmountable grief before Captain Rex and Goose materialized. There have been times for both my children when the tears and sobs have lasted a whole evening. They've looked like panic attacks. They've come and gone for months over the same thing.

And what if your child doesn't know what they feel? Well, you don't want to be telling them how they feel, but you could try offering a few possibilities to choose from. Embarrassment? Neutral? Shame? Boredom? Numbness? Anger? Whenever I list a choice of feelings and emotions, Wilf knows which one sits right. 'That's it!' There are feelings colour wheels online that you can print off for free if that helps to prompt ideas. Stick one up on the wall and get the whole family involved. And don't forget you can be lots of things at once. You can feel happy and sad at the same time, be ashamed and hopeful, or experience grief around one thing and simultaneously joy about another.

It once took several days for us to get to the bottom of an emotion that Wilf was feeling, when it suddenly occurred to me. Worthlessness? Yes. That hit home. He didn't have the word for that before, just knew he didn't see the point in living, but now he does know that word and the emotional feel behind it. Once he named it, we could talk about where it came from and shine a light on it.

Emotional literacy gives you agency in life and is empowering. It's one of the best things we can do with our children.

Name our own emotions out loud as we go along and help them to name theirs.

And the best part about this is that's really all there is to it. If you're having conversations about emotions and naming them. Bang! You're nailing it. So that's a load off right there.

Feelings aren't there to be solved. We're brought up to think that happiness and joy are feelings to be felt and that the others – anger, shame, sadness, grief, etc. – are in some way to be resolved and dealt with, soothed away, pushed aside or squashed down.

But feelings are information for us about us. They are never about another person or the thing that's happened. They help us learn about ourselves with that person or in that situation. If your child is angry, is this because a boundary has been crossed? Is this information for them about who to trust and who to keep at arm's length? Has there been an injustice? Have they not had a need met? Do they feel out of control? Or is there shame below the anger?

You can ask your child, 'What do you think this feeling is telling you?' There's no right or wrong answer. If they say 'I don't know' or something random just go with it. All you are trying to achieve is to leave them asking themselves that question each time they feel something. Even if most of the time they have no answer. One day they will.

Anger is a funny one. I grew up with a psychotherapist mum.

I remember her clearly telling me that anger was sometimes anger (it's a protective response we feel when someone has crossed a boundary we've set in some way) but was also usually a few steps away from tears. She taught me that when people get angry, underneath they are often afraid, insecure, embarrassed, ashamed, frustrated or feeling inadequate as well. I didn't believe her at first. It sounded preposterous. Can't a person just be angry? But as the years went on, I saw it was true. So, when my children present with anger, I always try to look beyond it to what lies underneath. Is it a crossed boundary or is it the most acceptable (to them) version of fear, shame, etc.?

If you or your kids are neurodiverse, it's likely that emotions do feel big, and this may show up in an explosive meltdown, dysregulated behaviours, a withdrawal or numbing. When my son was going through a hard few years, I thought he was angry about a lot. Everything seemed to be expressed with anger: swearing, shouting, turning over tables and chairs at school, ripping down a display and walking off. I think this is because anger is more socially acceptable than fear. Society teaches boys to keep any emotions in that might lead to them being seen as weak and encourages them to be physical and angry instead.

Schools and mental health teams often talk about 'managing emotions' and for me there's always this feeling that they're trying to resolve or deal with emotions to make them socially acceptable and smaller so that the learning day might continue.

But if feelings are for feeling, and they are big and messy, and they sometimes feel never ending, how can you move forwards in your day?

After we named some of the really painful feelings, like shame, we talked.

'Shame is so hard,' said Wilf, one day. 'It's worse than sadness.'

'Yeah. I know what you mean... It feels horrible.' And then, 'Does it feel any better for having shared it? Even a small bit, like 1% better?'

'Yeah. It's weird because you think that saying it out loud is going to make it feel worse, but it doesn't. Not being alone with it any more makes it so much better. It's the last thing you want to do and then you do it and it's such a relief. It doesn't go away but it's easier.'

We thought about that for a moment, and then I added, 'picking a trusted person to share it with is important, I guess. Someone that won't throw it back at you later. I imagine shining an actual torch onto it and it not being as dark and grizzly as you thought. When you see it in the light, some of its power goes and it's just this thing that you're dealing with, but it's not something to fear any more.'

When Wilf struggled with a big emotion, we named it, shone a light on it and watched it. Sometimes we gave it a number out of ten to see how strong it was and then later saw if it had grown, shrunk or stayed the same in intensity. We didn't try and fix it. We found our soft landing place for the afternoon/ day/week and we consciously upped our connection. The big emotion passed like a storm, and soon there were blue skies again.

When Wilf was younger, he had a phase of loving graffiti art, and we bought a load of pens to practise the cool writing in. We drew big feeling words like 'shame' and then a flashlight shining on it and made a scrapbook of them.

SOMETHING PRACTICAL TO TRY...

Practise naming your emotions with your child. What are you feeling right now? What's behind it? What else is there? Each of you pick one and draw it big and fancy or small and spindly, whatever fits! Try and make the style and colour how the word feels to you. You can add a flashlight above shining down if you feel like it.

Indirect Messages of Love

A mum I met along the way told me that sometimes she finds herself wanting to say something heartfelt to her autistic daughter, but she knows it will be too confrontational and she'll be told to go away. The truth is the mum's words are met with so many big emotions that it is uncomfortable to hear. If that mum attempts to say how much she loves her daughter face-to-face, with good eye contact, it's very possible that her daughter will feel accosted by her mother's energy, emotions and presence and her own thoughts of how she should respond. What that looks like is her daughter finding it too intense to hear and shouting or pushing her mum out of the bedroom and shutting the door.

During the teenage years this somehow becomes harder again because it's part of a teenager's brain development to push against you and to find out who they are in the world outside of your rules and expectations. It's a time for becoming more emotionally independent.

This mum told me that she had been texting and sending little videos occasionally to her daughter to let her know that she was loved in a less direct way and that this was working really well for their relationship. I just loved the thought of this. It's looking at the situation imaginatively.

Why not leave them a casual note by their lunch? Or send them a silly gif (animation), a voice recording or a few seconds of video. Yes, they'll say you're cringy, but they will also feel your love. Being less direct and allowing your child to open it in their own time can, in the end, be a more considered approach. And they won't feel watched whilst you say the thing. Instead, they have time to process and respond if they wish to.

Points to consider:

- Be aware of your tone of voice. Try smiling, if recording your voice.

- What is their learning style? If reading is a struggle, make it auditory.

- Keep it short.

- Positive vibes only. No arguing your point. That should always happen in person.

- Sometimes a silly meme or funny video you know they'd appreciate can be a great repair after an argument or difficult day. But you shouldn't throw repairs in unless you've listened and apologized or taken responsibility for your parts of the conflict.

- Don't expect a response.

I find that as my children get older and are starting to go off into the world for longer periods of time, I'm full of fear some days. It's important that teenagers take calculated risks to gain independence, but it's scary for a mum like me, who's been holding everything together so tightly. I worry, and the temptation is to tell them all my fears so that they can somehow avoid those things happening to them. But I've tried this (unconsciously!), and it just spreads all my anxiety to them. Delivering all my little parcels of fear at their feet is not helpful or connecting. It's not empowering them. They need to know that I trust them and think they're capable.

In these circumstances I meditate, visualizing love from me to them and layers of protective energy. It's somewhere to put all that love and concern when it's not appropriate to burden them with it.

PAUSE AND REFLECT

What unspoken message to your child rests in your heart?
Write it down.

. . . .

. . . .

. . . .

. . . .

. . . .

. . . .

. . . .

. . . .

SOMETHING PRACTICAL TO TRY...

Choose between note, audio message and video
message based on their best way of taking in information (not what's easier for you).

Write or record a short message from the heart, keeping your tone of voice light and loving.

Send your offering of love to your child. Do not look
for validation or a response (although you can check
they got it after some time has passed). The gift is in

how good it feels to express yourself without stressing them out.

If your child is away from home or does not respond positively to the other forms of indirect messages, try a meditation. I've got it covered. You can listen to my meditation created specifically for these types of moments on the Insight Timer app. I made it when my 19-year-old daughter was away in Bali.

Rewriting the Story

The messages our children consciously and unconsciously receive from school include: sit still; work harder; you're being lazy; you're not doing enough; you're not good enough; you're failing; you need to try harder; stop messing about; you're disruptive; you're bad; you find school hard; stop making a fuss; stop being you; squeeze yourself to fit our rules and expectations; sit still some more; be quiet.

I did not take Wilf to parents' evenings to be lectured and shamed in front of me. I used those moments to try and build rapport with the teacher and communicate need, to brainstorm ideas for things we could try between us. After the first few, I stopped reading his school reports to him. They try to keep them upbeat with a balance of encouragement and stretch, but, honestly, I don't think they were helpful for him to hear. They often brought me to tears.

My husband Steve had had many terrible reports at school. He said that the worst part had been the shame of giving them to his dad to read. He'd hidden them sometimes. His dad got angry. Both the teachers and his parents acted like Steve was deliberately not trying to do well at school. He was being told off and shamed for something he had absolutely no control over, and he ended up constructing a rebellious persona to make this fit. Wilf didn't hide his reports. They were always crumpled in his bag. He had no interest in them.

So, I began giving him just the highlights, a short and sweet summary and sometimes added in things I wished the teacher had noticed or said. He abruptly left primary at the beginning of Year 6 and at the end of that bumpy year I wrote my own report.

From then on, in school or out, I wrote my own. It was a great way to see all the things he'd experienced and learned when everyone else was telling him he wasn't learning anything. Of course he was! He wasn't attending lessons or filling in worksheets, but he was always following his curiosity. He had a lot of interests and asked a lot of questions. The reports focused on him as a whole, not just on his academic abilities, which are such a small sliver of what makes up a person.

I also went on to write a ten-page Word document that gave a true account of Wilf's primary school experience. In part

I wrote that for me, to give myself a chance to process it all. But it's also there for Wilf, when he's an adult and wants to make sense of his early years. Perhaps he will have children one day and want to unpick and process the school experience as an adult. There's a lot of trauma there to be healed.

I describe the pre-school and school, what he liked doing in each class, his hobbies, favourite TV shows, friends, birthday parties and memorable trips, Halloween costumes and projects. I recount funny stories and explain the difficulties he had rationally, giving the reasons behind them. I describe his teachers from my adult point of view, and then the way in which things spiralled into leaving that school, but I don't sensationalize those parts. I state them calmly and factually.

It's very therapeutic to set down the facts, the highs and lows. If you enjoy writing, I fully recommend it. It took me several hours over several days, but it was so satisfying. Other options are to make a voice recording, a video or lists of highlights from each school year.

Only do it if you want to though. If that task sounds overwhelming, you have my permission not to do it! Or to just start now, from this year. Or to look at this year's end-of-year report and form a short and positive summary to relay to your child.

If your child is home-educated, it's still a lovely way to celebrate the passing days and take stock of all they've done.

Look back through the calendar and phone photos for prompts.

I include: trips; friends; milestone events, like a sleepover, getting a new pet, etc.; holidays; special interests and what we learned; a situation or big emotional moment he coped with and how; books we read together or Wilf was listening to on audio; ways in which he earned money; stuff like how he let go of old toys by selling them to make money for new toys; what he learned to cook and do; how he spent his down time and what he learned from that; and any outdoor sports we've done. I do mention one or two difficult situations if they were big, but framed as a challenge that was got through.

Resilience Is Bullshit

From the early days, I always had this inner knowing that school wasn't a good fit for Wilf. By the end of primary school, I was fairly sure that it was a very unhealthy environment for him, and yet I still went through the motions of placing him elsewhere, getting an Education, Health and Care Plan (EHCP), then another more specialist placement. I'm not sure any of that did him good. We were searching for somewhere that he could fit in, meet friends, be part of a community, give us time to get work done each day, maybe get some qualifications and, looking back, to stay within our family culture and society's expectations.

The message I received from outside of myself was that you can have learning difficulties, but you still need to battle on and be victorious, to gain at least a few BTechs and a Duke of Edinburgh's Award award or do an apprenticeship. When none of that seemed possible, just attending somewhere where you were learning practical things and did outdoor ed was acceptable to others in my extended family. Other young men in our families (on both sides and going back generations) had struggled or done badly at school, but they'd managed to suck it up and stick it out, mostly leaving school with nothing more than a fear of being out of control and low self-esteem to show for it. They'd all done ok in life, and some had gone back and achieved some qualifications later on. Despite their experiences of suffering, they all bizarrely agreed with the cultural norm, that school was important and for the best.

My inner knowing that this path was wrong felt like a nervous tummy and a tight chest when I thought about trying to fit Wilf somewhere, with him, bless him, trying desperately to make each thing work when it just couldn't. He tried so many times. I remember one school saying that he needed to build flexibility and resilience through various schemes and activities, and thinking to myself that Wilf has got to be one of the most resilient boys I know. He is still showing up every day, hoping it will all fall into place and yet, deep down, knowing at the same time that it won't because the systems and adults around him were not using helpful approaches. Our society has somewhere along the line decided that quitting is always bad and sticking it out is always good.

What does resilience really mean? Asking children and young people to be resilient feels to me like coercion. It's what systems of power use to keep people doing what they want them to do. The government and our accepted culture promote keeping children in education at all costs. But really, at ALL costs? Even if that is an unhealthy environment for them personally or a bad school system in general that is no longer serving many modern-day kids?

Instead of celebrating 100% attendance we should be proud of the kids that listen to their bodies when they are sick or stressed or have their periods, that know or figure out what doesn't feel right to them and what isn't working for them. Because in 20 years' time they will not be the ones doing a job that makes them feel empty inside. Sometimes we need to honour and celebrate walking away. It feels brave and healthy to me.

It took me time to come to that conclusion; meanwhile at each new place I would be hopeful that the staff would have the experience, patience and expertise required and that maybe I could learn something from them, but I was always disappointed.

The last place, which received an immense amount of funding for Wilf, used a heady mix of coercive control, emotional manipulation, threats (of taking treats away like golden time and the end-of-term trip) and points systems. He was promised points for every class he attended, as if he'd suddenly be able to overcome all his difficulties to get them. They had a glass cabinet and would ask the children what they wanted, order it off Amazon and lock it in this cupboard of dreams that hardly anyone could access because if they could do all the things and follow a timetable and swallow all the worksheets, they wouldn't be there would they? They'd be at a regular school.

The alternative was home education, but that came with its own set of challenges. There was a financial implication for one: it would be hard for me to work, and all the things Wilf wanted to do cost money. Even art projects weren't simple. At the time, Wilf liked graffiti spray paints and Posca pens and fake Astroturf for his *Jurassic Park* diorama. He didn't want to play ping pong in the park every day.

The idea of trying to fill the days felt very tiring and like my life would feel smaller somehow, less free, as Wilf needed support to stay balanced throughout the day.

Glennon Doyle says that it's often the way that both paths are hard. As in... an unhappy, broken marriage is the wrong kind of hard even if it doesn't rock the boat but a divorce in that situation is the right kind of hard because it's truthful and freeing. Both are going to be hard, but one sets you off in a positive direction.

So, you pick the hard that feels right. The one that feels warm, true, centred and growthful even though it also feels hard. For us, Wilf being miserable and unsupported at school was a very hard path to bear. We were all full of tension and operating at capacity getting him there and communicating with the school on everything that went wrong, which was almost daily. Stepping out of the system and him being at home would also be extremely hard for many reasons. But in a heartbeat, I felt in my body that it was the right kind of hard.

There are always going to be people out there who think that parents of neurodiverse children (who have either shut down or become oppositional) are not setting firm boundaries or disciplining enough.

I think most of us started with stronger discipline and found it didn't make a difference. But honestly, how hard are you going to go? You don't want a controlling and abusive relationship with your child. Instead, you have to sense when your children need encouraging to step out of their comfort zone and when to respect their limits. If they are old enough, you can certainly ask them because every child wants to succeed where they can. Most of us are parenting our socks off.

There will be those who say stuff like, 'What doesn't kill us makes us stronger' or that 'tough love' is needed. But what are we teaching our kids when we push them towards places that don't feel safe and nurturing to them? Or doing things that aren't genuinely rewarding and meaningful? Is that really pampering or making healthy choices for your child?

We require our children to sit still for six hours of the day, be quiet, listen, write down notes, memorize, be highly controlled and to follow instructions and rules without question. It's probably not great for any of them, but when those individuals show signs of stress, anxiety and poor mental health because of it, does toughening up really seem like the best way forward?

We're asking them to follow the rules of society to ensure everyone around them feels comfortable even at the cost of high anxiety or depression. We require them to make themselves uncomfortable and stressed to remain in the confines of the norm, where everyone else can relax around them, knowing that they will come out of the sausage machine employable. One of the *best* parts of your neurodiverse child is that, more often than not, they can't comply with things that don't feel right. They push back and it's an honest and healthy reaction. That sausage machine is just a construct and it's not for them.

So… how do we listen to our inner knowing about whether to keep our child in school or at home, when there are all these other voices giving their opinions and making us doubt ourselves?

To make it feel less scary, I just think about the next step that feels right. So maybe you're in a provision that hasn't been working, and you've communicated with the staff and given feedback and they've listened. You've all tried to adapt the experience to meet your child where they are. You've given this time, but it's still not working. That's when I lean in to my knowing and ask myself can this ever be right for my child?

Or is this provision just structured in a way that cannot meet their needs? Are the staff just not the right personalities? Would my child be happier and safer at home or somewhere else?

After I've allowed my mind to explore what's going on, I quieten my thoughts. For this, a meditation or breathwork session can be helpful, but so can a solo stroll in the countryside. My mind is limited by my fears and by the cultural expectations that I've grown up with. So, I listen to my body. What does my heart say? What does my gut say?

When you follow your instincts there are no mistakes. You explore what feels right in the moment, and if in time you learn more about yourself and your children, and what feels right changes, then you explore the next step on the trail. One step at a time.

PAUSE AND REFLECT

Think of a time that you did not follow your instincts regarding your child. Describe what it felt like and what happened.

. . . .

. . . .

. . . .

. . . .

Write or talk aloud about a time when you did follow your inner knowing. What happened as a result of that?

. . . .

. . . .

. . . .

. . . .

What is your knowing telling you now about the right next step?

. . . .

. . . .

. . . .

. . . .

Society's Expectations

One of the most extraordinary things that this journey awakened in me was how much we live conforming unconsciously to the expectations of our family of origin, our community and the culture we've either been brought up in or that exists currently around us (or a blend of all of these!).

When your child, and therefore your family, hits a crisis point something has to give. If your child has extreme symptoms and behaviours, then it might be obvious to you and those around you that they cannot fit into the normal school journey. Other options and support may have been triggered early on, but most parents start off entering their child into the system, then problems arise when it gradually becomes apparent that the system maybe isn't a great fit for them. There will probably be years of trying to adapt the expectations and activities to help the child, and this may be enough for some to get through or even thrive. I suspect though that most parents reading this book have either painfully struggled to get their child through the education system (and even in a specialist school, that struggle still exists) or they have opted out and are flying solo because it just can't work.

When my son was nine or ten (the age that typically children start to conform with society's expectations if they haven't already), he had his first exclusion from school. Don't get me wrong, things had been getting progressively worse for years. He hated school. He cried and clung. He came home unbelievably tired with stories of punishments. No break today, had to do work over lunchtime, no golden time, stars taken off the star chart, shamed in front of the other children.

One teacher decided that he would have to stay late to complete the work, which meant me standing awkwardly, red-faced in the playground and being told he was being kept in in front of the other parents and children. I had to wait whilst every other child was collected until it was just me standing there alone. He hadn't done the work earlier because it was so noisy, he couldn't concentrate, he had no sensory input and the task felt too big and complicated with lots of steps on a worksheet. He found it harder than anyone else, and yet he was being made to stay longer and try harder. Another teacher (the headteacher) talked to the whole class in front of him. How does Wilf's disruption make you feel class? Is it difficult to work when he is banging his ruler on the table and saying his repetitive words? (Both things his brain was doing to try and keep himself awake.) The class, of course, agreed with the headteacher because authority figures must be obeyed, and anyway the disruptions probably were annoying. I think she was trying to shame him into 'behaving' in a more appropriate way, but of course he had no control over his behaviours and just felt angry and embarrassed.

Make yourself fit. These are the lessons we are taught at school. Children were taught them several hundred years ago, and children are still taught them today:

- Be co-operative.

- Sit still.

- Be quiet and listen.

- Write down facts.

- Memorize the facts.

- Work towards qualifications in order to have the best life.

- Qualifications = job = money = success.

- Be as productive as you can be doing things that don't interest you.

- Decide what career you'd like to have and aim for it.

- Follow the rules.

- Obey figures in authority.

- Look as much like everyone else as you can.

- If none of this feels right, try harder to achieve it.

- You're only as good as your grade.

- Measure yourself against the others around you.

- If you're not getting good grades, it's probably because you're lazy or don't care.

You can just about get away with not being academically strong if you are sporty, musical or arty, but you have to excel in whatever it is that you lean towards.

The current compulsory, state-funded education system was made widespread in the UK in the Victorian era to create a workforce that could follow instructions, co-operate and do repetitive work. It's a relatively new concept within the history of civilization. Before it existed, trades were handed down from father to son or in apprenticeships to those with the right aptitudes. People responded to what they were good at within their community. There have always been teachers, hunters, gatherers, farmers, healers, mystics, leaders, builders, cooks and creatives/inventors. So, really, education should be based on getting to know yourself, your strengths, weaknesses, abilities, likes and dislikes. What would be meaningful and satisfying to you? What would feel gruelling day after day and what would feel natural and fulfilling?

Neither of my children (one boy and one girl) fitted the education system for different reasons. One tried her best to for years and it nearly broke her. Her school's motto was 'Live Life to the Full'. It was laughable because you literally couldn't do anything except schoolwork all day and all evening. They were cutting out creative subjects left, right and centre too. At school she was about as far away from being able to live life to the full as she could have been. In fact, the motto just added more pressure. Do all that we ask you to do AND make sure your life is fulfilling.

The other child also tried very hard but was quicker to say no. Both showed remarkable resilience in the face of struggle and yet were constantly told they were not resilient enough.

I was slow to notice the problems for my daughter. I thought her brain was like my brain. I thought her conformity was capacity. I feel guilty for not listening, but I didn't know then what I know now. We must live with the fact that I didn't choose what was best for her (until 16 when I gave all choice and control over to her) because I didn't believe I had a choice. You can only parent with the tools and knowledge you have at the time.

One day when I was called to pick my son up early, he gave me a tear-stained, crumpled exclusion note. This small child burrowed his face into my skirt as the headteacher told him this exclusion was extremely serious and would go on his formal record. She made it sound like a criminal record, like he was now marked in some way, his future held in question. When his face appeared, it was terrified. I was livid with their treatment of the situation, but I didn't look at the woman and the other people in the staff room. I got down on Wilf's level and took the paper from him and put it away in my bag. I asked him if he was ok and ready to go home? I gave him a hug and rubbed his back. I didn't care what he'd done in that moment; he was the most distressed I'd ever seen him, and I responded to that.

As we walked down the school drive Wilf said, 'I hate my life. I just want to be dead.' I was crying inside hearing this, but I tried to remain calm. 'It sounds like you've had a really stressful day.'

'Mum, I just don't know who I am there, at school. I can't find myself.' He was telling me that he was so deep in his stress responses and so dysregulated that even he didn't know why he was acting the way he was acting. He couldn't feel good about himself or even neutral. He didn't recognize himself. He said he wanted to die, but when we talked about this further, he just wanted it all to stop, all the suffering to go away.

The next day I de-registered him from school. It involved printing out a template off the internet, signing it and handing it in. Nothing more. No one rang from the school. No one rang from the authorities for months. No one cared. And it felt empowering.

For the next six weeks we did simple things. We baked and went to the aquarium. Wilf still repeated a lot of words noisily like a vocal tic, and everything stressed him out. I could feel his energy fizzing next to me and he was hypervigilant. It took several months for him to unwind.

When I handed that letter in, it was the first taste of choosing something different. We would go on to explore other terrible options, but that day, despite all the advice and judgement I knew we'd get from concerned family, friends and the community, all I felt was relief, a deep knowing inside of me that this was the right thing for Wilf. Ok, it wasn't all I felt. I also felt fear, shame, a loss and a sense of grief. We'd been a large active part of the school community, being on the board of governors and the PTA. Wilf was in his last year and now wouldn't get to go on residential or have the leavers' assembly. I felt judged by the other parents and excluded when we saw them in the park. But these feelings didn't last. And none of that was worth the cost to Wilf's mental health and self-esteem.

Once I knew what it felt like to say 'no more' and what a

relief it was to act on it, it has been a guideline in my life ever since, and the sense I have of following my inner knowing, my ability to recognize it and my courage to act on it have strengthened. My knowing centres around my heart and the line across my chest at about that level. I feel a distant hum of hope, a brightness of mind and my feet fully planted on the floor. I feel relieved, at peace and energized at the same time.

PAUSE AND REFLECT

Can you write down a time in which you defied society's expectations for your child? What did that feel like in your body? (The best way to explore this can be to quieten your mind for a few minutes, close your eyes and picture the scene. Then scan down your body from head to feet and see if there are any sensations or tensions there.)

If you haven't yet defied expectations, which one would you most like to push past for the sake of your child? Can you imagine how it might feel in your body?

. . . .

. . . .

Write down all your fears about defying society and choosing what you think is best for your child.

. . . .

. . . .

. . . .

. . . .

Then write down all your fears about not acting on your knowing and following the social norms.

. . . .

. . . .

. . . .

. . . .

A Wide Open Space

One day my son Wilf and I were walking to the local super-market and he began talking about wanting a bigger room to store all his Lego® in. He is an enthusiastic collector of the first degree, and I was saying that we can't really give him a bigger room and that we can't afford to move house (his next question) because I don't work right now, not in the traditional sense where I'm earning a monthly income.

Years ago I started freelance copywriting to work flexibly, so that when the school holidays came round I could be there in the day and do my hours in the evenings. This helped when Wilf was in and out of school too, because it became very hard to use the time he was out of the house.

I never knew when the school were going to ring to ask me to come and pick him up or tell me he'd jumped the gate and was running in the direction of home, or could I talk to him please as he was refusing to do anything. Once when he was in Year 7 or 8 of an oddball independent school, I was asked to come over and talk to him in the staff room watched by several teachers, where, having refused lessons, he'd been given the task of moving stacks of books and didn't want to do that or anything else. They were, like, let's watch you deal with this, and I did, calmly and cheerfully with slightly pink cheeks, whilst also wondering how this would have worked if I'd been a lawyer or a nurse with a shift to cover.

On a typical day I would just have sat down at the computer after the hell of a morning school run, and then it would take my brain time to still, to get back into where I had left off in the project or task I was working on. I'd just get there and then the school would ring. Or I wouldn't be able to get there because I was worried that the school *might* ring or the phone actually would ring and I'd jump, a flash of adrenaline streaking through my body to discover my mum on the other end asking if I'd got him into school ok.

This situation got worse in the next school, where he started his transition at two days a week and never transitioned. In fact, there were many days in which he didn't go in or had to come home, and weeks at a time when he would refuse school, so my work petered down to nothing much. He was at home so much, his mental health in tatters, that I couldn't really get any other job and all my time was spent supporting him or trying to manage my own mental health as I navigated the form-filling, appointments and phone calls it all seemed to entail.

Currently Wilf's not in school at all, so I was explaining to him (as we trailed the aisles looking for comfort) that we couldn't just buy a bigger house and get a bigger mortgage, because I'm at home. And he thought about that and said something along the lines of, 'I don't want to be at home needing support in a way that means you can't work.' Despite what it may look like to teachers, no child wants to fall outside of the system. They all, without exception, want to be successful and liked by staff and peers. It's only when they can't meet the system's expectations that they opt out, losing a lot of self-esteem along the way.

I started to reassure him, horrified that he thought of himself as somewhat of a burden. I started saying things like, 'Children who go to school and have parents that go to work – they also have difficulties. They also have stressful days and things they can't have – like bigger bedrooms – and they also have to work flexibly around their living space. It's just a different set of problems. A different life and a different set of problems.'

But as I was saying this to him, my brain in full TED Talk mode, scrambling for the positive, I had this sudden, huge realization: Wilf being at home had left this wide open space, and we hadn't even looked up and seen it.

We began excitedly to talk about this, how when you take away school, the one-size-fits-all education system and society's expectations for our life, what you are left with is a wilderness of a week, which we had tried to add schoolish structure to at first. We'd failed at that and kind of slumped into snacking and screen time and moment-by-moment balancing our mental health. But we were actually free to fill that space with whatever we wanted, both of us, with anything we could imagine for ourselves.

As we ate cheese pretzels under a tree in the supermarket carpark, the sun came out. People came and went in the spaces near to us, going about their day, and we just sat on the grass enjoying our freedom. For a split second it seemed as if all of life was rushing around us getting through its task list and we alone were standing still, to one side of it, watching.

I'd spent years willing and cajoling Wilf into school, but that day for the first time Wilf's school refusal felt like a massive, life-altering gift for both of us. I said it out loud. If he was going to school every day, I would be earning money in a job that paid the bills and I wouldn't be focusing on what soothes me, what brings me to life, shaping our week consciously. It's very possible that that job would be mundane and unfulfilling, because most of the work I did before fell into that category. And I probably wouldn't have the time and space to be as creative as I wanted to be.

I reminded my son that writing was my passion, and that our

time at home allowed me to get up early and write before his day even began because there were no packed lunches and school runs and homework.

And recently I'd had an idea for this book. I wanted to write a book that would feel like a friend rather than an expert to parents in the same situation, so that we could all feel together and less alone. And I wanted to support my family financially using my creative skills and in a way that was meaningful to me, in a way that brought me to life and gave this freedom to others in our situation. I wouldn't have had the time and headspace to process our experience if he was at school and we were both coping with that.

He really got it. His face lit up.

And all at once we were looking at our future from a completely different perspective. The feeling ran right through my body. From a place of what if... What if I wrote a book and he made Lego® animations and ran his cat-sitting business and researched WW2? What if, despite the ridiculously low income, we created the life we wanted to have? What if, instead of not managing to find the next school or fit the system, we were creating a better, more precious existence for both of us, for all of us as a family?

It can be scary to look beyond what is offered and to step off the system's conveyor belt. It will possibly be met with fear or judgement from your extended family or friends. Some parents do it from the start of the difficulties, way back in primary school; others need to experience what's on offer and see if their child can fit into any of it.

But eventually there is a (growing) group of families whose children's needs remain inadequately supported by their learning centre. A mix of conflicting diagnoses and personalities that need such flexibility to succeed that it blows Ofsted's tiny mind. Or the Board of Education for those in America. Any standardized place cannot meet the child where he/she/they are AND tick curriculum boxes.

And stepping off doesn't mean that it all becomes easier, because it doesn't. On the daily, it's not easy. There are lots of problems: all the dysregulation; the family dynamics; people up to their full capacity, not coping. But we would be dealing with those things anyway, in different forms.

Sometimes having a neurodiverse child is an amazing opportunity to step out of the system and the unconscious conforming into a wide open space. If you have come to this point or can see it within reach, I encourage you to embrace it.

But you don't need to be freestyling it to enjoy and complete this journal. We've tried it all. This book is for frazzled parents of neurodiverse kids whether they are in a mainstream or specialist school, home-educated or doing their own sweet thing.

PAUSE AND REFLECT

Let's begin by unearthing ideals and expectations that you grew up with. What were you taught to believe is a good education?

. . . .

. . . .

. . . .

. . . .

What achievements and qualifications have you been trained to believe are essential for success in modern-day life?

. . . .

. . . .

. . . .

. . . .

What do you think of as being successful in life? Question your first answers and dig deep for the most essential, core things.

. . . .

. . . .

. . . .

. . . .

Make a detailed list of as many things (appropriate to their learning abilities) as you can think of that it would be useful for your child to know, experience or learn to do before becoming an adult. Then circle your top five.

. . . .

. . . .

. . . .

. . . .

When I asked myself what success really meant to me I realized it was loving well and being loved, a connected family, healthy relationships, staying true to who I am, building my self-worth, living creatively, living a life where I feel alive and having enough money to cover the basics.

Guess what. It didn't involve GCSEs. Or my ridiculously niche degree in South Asian Studies with Hindi.

Collaborative Solutions

Most neurodiverse children are very bright. They don't all fit into one area of genius (savants) as represented on TV and in books, but in my experience they're often very inventive, good at thinking outside the box and ruthless negotiators. So, when you have a problem with something, sometimes THEY are your greatest asset.

But regardless of intellect, all children should be involved in working out solutions collaboratively. In *The Explosive Child* by Dr Ross W. Greene (a very useful read despite its off-putting title), Dr Greene says that when a child has come up with something themselves, they are far more likely to try it with an open mind. It may involve you explaining why some ideas won't work (keep your tone of voice neutral, reasonable and breezy, remember) and sometimes trying out some of their ideas so that they can see exactly how it won't work before resorting to a different solution. Be respectful in this process. Exasperated 'I told you so's' will get you nowhere and break rapport. If they have no idea, give them a reasonable range of possible solutions and let them pick which one they want to try first.

Won't clean their teeth? Find out why. Get curious. It could be they have PDA (pathological demand avoidance), and some days have higher levels of anxiety that stop them being able to follow demands. Perhaps it's not PDA, but they are sick of the nagging and being asked to do things so are just automatically pushing back, or it could be a sensory thing. If you're lucky, it might be something super-simple like the toothpaste is too strong in taste or the bristles too hard. Could they choose a softer brush, a fruity paste or even rub their teeth with paste on their finger on more difficult days?

If your child was able to clean their teeth without the rigmarole of being cajoled, I'm pretty sure they would. No one wants fillings and rotten teeth. If it's a sensory issue, would holding something on their lap that vibrates help or cleaning the teeth under a weighted blanket? Is a manual brush better than a vibrating toothbrush or vice versa? Would once a day be as good as it gets and lessen conflict?

If you suspect they have PDA, asking them to clean their teeth makes the job even less likely to be actioned. There will be times when they can't even get themselves to do things they *want* to do. Lowering anxiety is key to this dynamic, alongside knowing when to let things go and prioritizing the most important things.

And find ways with your child to get round the situation themselves. You can research ideas and suggest them, like imagining the teeth are cars in a car wash with people inside, mumbling about how long it's taking. That idea was given by an autistic person on a comments thread, who was explaining how they have to get around themselves to do it. A little imagination can go a long way. Any fresh idea to distract the brain is worth a try if your child thinks it's worth a try. Give the choice and control to your child where it is safe to do so.

And for your own sanity, let go of the things you can't change or are turning into a battle. Focus on rapport and come back to them on a better day. You're not a bad parent if you offer your child reminders to clean their teeth and they don't act on them. They are not going to look back at the age of 35 and ask why you didn't stand over them until they cleaned their teeth. They were there with you. They will know why it didn't happen.

In our house, I managed to solve the teeth dilemma by putting the control firmly back in the children's court. I explained what would happen if they didn't clean their teeth. I told them that it worried me because we only have one set of adult teeth... yadda yadda. Then I explained that these were their teeth we were discussing. My teeth would be just fine in my old age because I cleaned them. As this was their teeth, there was nothing that I could do. This is an example of standing beside the demand. One kid shrugged and one asked for help, and I replied saying that I didn't like the twice daily battles and I was happy to let the teeth cleaning go.

Eventually we settled on the solution that I would give one or two calm and neutral reminders because they forget. After that it's down to them. And I stuck to this whilst they were pre-teen. I reminded. Nothing happened. It was always a case of 'I'll do it in a minute/later'. I reminded a second time and pleasantly said that I wouldn't be reminding again. It was on them. If I got the 'I'll do it later' reply again, I also calmly pointed out that that didn't work since they often forgot later so they might need to stop what they are doing and set a timer. Sometimes the teeth weren't done. It really was on them because I had bigger fish to fry. But the daily battles at least stopped.

Next time you want to change something that isn't working well, ask your child what they would do if they were the parent, and whatever that is, try it. If it doesn't help, let them process this and then ask again, 'That didn't seem to solve the problem. What do you think we should try next?'

Codependency in a Neurodiverse Family

Oof! This is a tricky one. In its simplest terms, a codependent relationship is when one person needs the other person, who in turn, needs to be needed. It's two people who have become enmeshed.

But here's the thing. The most commonly held image of a codependent relationship is one partner who's either unpredictably explosive or an alcoholic and the other who is dancing around them, never confronting them or letting the person's anger or alcoholism upset the other areas of their lives. Instead of letting the person with the rage or addiction see the results of the suffering they are causing to themselves and to those they love, letting the cards fall where the cards are going to fall, the partner is on constant alert for damage control. They are catching and snatching up those cards.

There's an imbalance with one under-functioning due to mental illness, addictions, immaturity, irresponsibility or underachievement and the other over-functioning. And it's a style of relationship that can be passed down generationally. If your parent has over- or under-functioned in their marriage or parental style, you are more likely to unconsciously feel familiar with that set-up and reproduce it in your own home.

The issues are not discussed, and the over-functioning partner will try to steer the alcoholic into better choices in a passive way, always trying to be in control of an uncontrollable situation. The whole family ends up tiptoeing around the difficult or under-functioning person. They don't argue back. They are too scared of the alcoholic's angry outbursts. They don't question their choices. They stay small. But what that is unwittingly doing is enabling this behaviour to continue. What looks like a one-sided problem is, in reality, a two-sided problem.

Believe it or not though, the most common sort of codependent relationship is not alcoholic marriages, it's between parent and child. In a codependent parent–child relationship, the lines between protective and obsessive, and engaged and over-involved, are often blurred beyond recognition. The caregiver/care-receiver nature of a parent–child relationship makes codependency really difficult to detect.

Some parents in unhappy partnerships or single parents can hang out and talk to their kids in place of a partner. They act more like friends than parents, looking for emotional support and advice from their children or for company when doing their hobbies. (Don't get me wrong, it's not a problem to share the joy of a hobby with your child – but it is a problem if you only ever do this with your child, and get annoyed when they are busy or not in the mood, because you don't have other friends you can go with or don't like to do it alone. The child should have no pressure, spoken or unspoken, to come with you.)

It's also easy to over-function when trying to safeguard your child against danger. Extreme protectiveness causes low self-esteem and stops children learning about themselves and developing skills. Some parents are scared their children might fail or not be prepared for life, so they constantly criticize and re-do the imperfect things the child has had a go at. Or they never let the child have a go, jumping in before they've had a chance. As you can imagine, the child ends up trying less, learning less and not reaching out of their comfort zone, which leads to anxiety and disempowerment.

When I read all this about codependency, I recognized a lot of things that we as parents were doing. What was confusing was how not to over-function when your child is sometimes under-functioning. The books don't talk about that. And of course, an over-functioner will always assume the other person is under-functioning as they unconsciously get value out of being needed in that way, so this is an opportunity to really inspect yourself for what is true.

Here are some starting points:

- Do you invite your child to hang out or do stuff with you like cycling, rock climbing, etc. because you can't be bothered to organize a friend coming along or are socially awkward? Be as honest as you can with yourself.

- Do you jump in to tie shoelaces or help with the baking because it'll be quicker or you don't want a mess?

- Do you pack your child's bag because they will forget stuff and get into trouble?

- Are you involved in all the drama your child has in their friendships, needing every little update or checking their messages?

- If your child is rejected, do you feel it personally as if the rejection is happening to you?

- Do you lose your temper as a way of getting your child to change their behaviours?

- Do you do their homework or help with projects to the

extent that you created the thing they will be marked on?

- If someone in the house loses something, do you immediately help to look for it?

- Are you prepared to let them take risks?

- Are you able to watch them suffer when they get things wrong or don't have what they want?

Blimey, it's hard! My husband and I can probably hold our hands up to most of the above over the years. But as I said, those lines are very blurred. And I think with neurodiverse children the lines are even more blurry, because those young people have areas where they have lagging skills, so over time it's natural that we've stepped in to support more fully. Of course we did. It makes sense.

But add to this the fact that your young person might feel very out of control within the school system, and out of control possibly in their behaviours and responses to things that happen. That feeling of being out of control means that they're often coming from a disempowered base. The thing they most need to grow is a feeling of capability. The more we step in, the more our children feel incapable, and this can cause a whole lot of anxiety.

But please don't be hard on yourself. This dynamic builds invisibly. Perhaps you're still packing their school bag long past when other parents have stopped, because your kids are distressed if they forget things and you want to give them the best chance of having a successful day. Maybe you help with homework because they have nothing left in them when they come home from school and you don't want them to get a detention. You might make breakfast because they are too stressed to think about eating. Before you know it, your acts of love and care are propping that person up so much that it's become the norm. It's a Saturday and they're 14 and you're still pouring the cereal.

I think the main reasons I have acted in these ways are because I often felt my children were dealing with so much just getting themselves to school. The idea of adding other tasks that they found difficult (due to time-blindness or lagging executive skills) but I could take care of in a flash seemed crazy, so I just did them. I couldn't stand the idea that if they were late to school or had forgotten their lunch or homework or PE kit, they would suffer even more than I knew they were already suffering just by being there.

And I don't regret those actions. However, there were then times when we were all under a lot less stress, fewer time constraints, lower stakes, and I still kept stepping up because that's what my role and our dynamic had become. I believed they were acts of love and feared judgement from my in-the-future, grown-up kids. What would they say if they looked back and saw that I'd just been watching them struggle whilst I got on with my life? But what this meant is that they hadn't strengthened those skills along the way, learning through the suffering and so just looked to me to take over. It had led to my teenage daughter feeling anxious and disempowered.

I needed to learn to differentiate, stepping forward when it was appropriate and then stepping back when that was more appropriate.

It's the same with most teenagers. A teenager will show signs of wanting to become independent, and, as parents, our whole job is to support their growing independence so that one day they can go out into the world and function on their own. We want that for them, right? But then, when they do all the things that lead to this – take risks, have secrets, lie to us, rebel, fail to get up for their part-time job, fall short at a lot of things – we can't bear it. But that's our job. To bear it all because when they experience getting things wrong, it allows them to learn and grow.

You've basically got to be prepared and able to see your child suffer and allow them the time and space to re-balance. Of course, you're there in moments of complete crisis, but as a kind and loving, non-judgemental homebase. You listen and nurture. You let them feel your calm so that their nervous system can listen in to your nervous system and remember. You speak kindly to them so that they can develop compassion for themselves. You remind them of all the situations in which they've stepped up, dealt with hard things and lived on.

Typically, there was a time when if one of my children came

to me with a problem, I reacted quickly. I thought of all the ways I could help. If they couldn't find something, I dropped what I was doing and I searched the house because I was the person who knew where everything was and could find things the best. But these small problems were taking up all of my day and taking me away from the tasks I wanted to do, from my own 'sense of self' life I was trying create, beyond my role as a mother.

So now, when faced with a problem, I take a few moments to consider whether it requires my action or whether my action would be disenabling. If you've been waiting for it – this is the key part of the chapter that is going to make your life EASIER.

A lost sock, a passed deadline, hungry for a snack, a present for a friend, needs to pack a bag... as they get older, these are not my problems to solve. My job is to just listen sympathetically and nod. 'Yeah, that sounds tough. What are you going to do?' or 'What do you think you'll try next?' Jen Hatmaker in her podcast *For the Love* calls this letting the cards fall where the cards are going to fall and has reminded me of a well-known mantra: 'Not my circus'. This has been monumental in reminding me that I don't always need to jump in.

When your child is faced with a problem and they come to you with it, there are four possible pathways for you to respond:

1. You resolve the problem yourself, going over their

heads. (In other words you find their favourite top, wash their going-out outfit, message their friend to say they are being unreasonable, talk to their teacher or their boss, pay off their debt, etc.)

2. You give them advice.

3. You give them a listening ear.

4. You give them comfort in the form of a hug, some nourishing food, a walk together, etc., finding out what they need to feel comfort by asking the right questions.

Number one is not helpful. It's over-functioning and will be detrimental to their development and your relationship with them. The other three are all valid, but ask them. So often we go to advice first, drawing from our own experiences because we are trying to relate to and make sense of their dilemma. But this isn't very helpful for them and will evoke a lot of eye-rolling or a trance-like state. Nine times out of ten they just want to be listened to, to have a moan or a rant. They know what they should do next, or they figure it out whilst talking. I've asked my daughter to point out kindly when I am giving unwanted advice (the answer: ALL OF THE TIME) and am trying to get into the habit of asking at the beginning of the conversation what she needs from me. It's made our relationship so much better and there's really not much to it.

So next time someone in your family comes to you upset, ask them what they need – advice, a listening ear or comforting? If they require action – can you bat it back to them? And if they need advice – it isn't your job to provide a solution. Like any good counsellor or teacher worth their weight knows, your job is simply to ask the right questions that allow the young person to explore the situation and come to their own conclusions. They may well decide to try something that you know won't work. Let them try that and see. Let those cards fall so that they can see the consequences and learn.

Basically, I'm saying do less. This journal is about making our lives easier after all! No really, your neurodiverse child needs to build a growing sense of their capabilities to feel ok in the world, and that does require you to step back as much as you possibly can and to be growing your own capacity to watch them suffer and struggle at times. When I feel like my energy, love, care and concern need to go somewhere, I re-direct them. I meditate sending that child love and pro-tective layers in a way that won't disrupt their sense of self, I help re-style their rooms, cook a favourite meal, plan a birthday treat or moment of connection. It helps.

An Extra Bit About Suffering

It's really, really hard to watch your child suffer. That's why we all jump in. But the thing to understand about suffering is that it's truthful.

When any of us distract ourselves from our suffering, when we take the edge off it with a glass of wine or two or by buying things or busying ourselves in work or other areas, we are not attending to a painful truth. This then becomes invisible, and the suffering continues long past when it should.

Suffering exists so that we move ourselves in a better direction that is healing. It's the edge of discomfort that makes us change our lives. If we constantly soothe ourselves rather than meet our actual needs, or attempt to soothe and distract our kids, we're taking away their motivation to change things.

For example, your child may have to feel lonely for a while to feel motivated enough to experience their social anxiety and still agree to meet a potential new friend. They may have to feel the depth of a meaningless life before they will give a few new activities a go, or before they can have a conversation about the types of things they might enjoy doing if the circumstances were right. They may fully hate their bodies before they can ask for help and step onto a journey of self-acceptance.

Things that might cause our kids to suffer:

- They can't have something they want.

- They can't do something they want to do.

- They have a physical or mental disability that frustrates or saddens them.

- They don't have the ability to achieve something they'd like to achieve.

- They are struggling with their friendship skills.

- They are lonely or feel rejected.

- They can't find meaning in their lives.

- They wish they could go to school and be like other children they know.

- They feel worthless.

- They have low self-esteem.

- They hate their bodies.

- They hate their brains.

- They are struggling with puberty or sexual feelings.

- They can't relate to their biological gender.

- They hate their diagnoses.

- They can't find peace and contentment.

- They've lost something they valued or someone they loved.

Many of those things are outside of our control. We can help our kids name their feelings and shine a light on them, but we often can't easily solve this stuff.

But what we can do is encourage them to explore the truth and express it creatively. Lots of famous people became known for their art, their music or their scientific break-throughs off the back of a childhood or teenage years of suffering because they lost a loved one, had a disability or didn't fit in.

Being creative is something great to role-model. Can you doodle your feelings? Create a mural in the garden? Noodle a song on the guitar? Write a journal? Put some beats together on GarageBand? Paint a motif on the back of a denim jacket? Posca pen your bedroom door or a pair of trainers? Could you leave tempting art supplies out for others in the family to have a go with?

But what if their suffering is serious? What if it's big and overwhelming and possibly life-threatening? What if they are harming themselves?

Well, that's not easy at all. And it can look like all sorts of things. Even not eating enough or overeating is self-harm.

The opposite of self-harm seems to me to be self-care and self-expression. Your child might need help growing that kind and compassionate voice inside their head, just like you did all those chapters ago. Ask them how they would speak to their toddler cousin or friend's younger sibling (try to land on some-one they might identify as cute and innocent) if that small child was hurt or upset. Help them form loving sentences and encourage them to say or write them to themselves.

Encourage them to explore their feelings, to name them, to express them with fashion and music and art of any kind. If they have feelings about the way you have loved them or parented them, listen with all your heart and don't interrupt. Their healing is at the centre of your healthy relationship.

There will be times when you sit in the darkness alongside them so that despite the suffering they don't feel alone.

But don't get stuck there. That's no use to them. You must continue to look after yourself even when to do so feels crazy. Especially then.

Author Cheryl Strayed, in her 'Dear Sugar' advice column, says, 'What is inside of your control is to say, "How do I make myself strong and brave and whole so that I can be that strong, brave, whole person that will be there for this person I love so much?"' And that goes back to the first part of this book – strengthening your sense of self, keeping yourself alive inside and taking care of your needs. Suffering and watching our loved ones suffer deplete us, but we're not going to be able to love them the way we want to love them if we're that wrung out.

It may feel weird and wrong when your child is in despair, but we absolutely need to attend to ourselves in the midst of it all. We need to have pockets of respite where we laugh and connect and find meaning in our own lives. Finding the things that nurture us and the things that make us stronger, braver, more whole.

Those are the things that will allow you to carry on being the parent that you need to be for your kids. The parent that can bear the pain and suffering and not fall apart. In doing all those things, you'll realize that some of it is just beyond your control and you can better bear that fact when you are centred in your own life experience.

That's love – having the strength to do those things, in order to bear the impossible situations you can't change.

Soul Teacher

The first time I felt a hint of the soul teacher Wilf would become for me was back when he was in primary school. He hadn't started refusing back then, although he was resisting a lot and refusing to do many things when he got there.

The teacher said to me, 'He won't do PE,' and I thought, of course he won't. It was the spring and the whole school was invested in learning their May Day ribbon dances. Wilf hates country dancing, more than he hates removing his bearded dragon's evil smelling poop from its vivarium. He can't follow sequences or remember them without a lot of effort and practice. The whole thing was tiring and embarrassing. It made sense to me.

'And he won't do French.' No, I guess that makes sense too. His dyslexia means he can't sound out the words or learn the vocab, and he's already struggling in English.

I'd been a goody-two-shoes at school. Obedient. Even now my knee-jerk response is to bow to authority figures and do what they say, even if it's out of line with my own needs. Having a child that said no and sometimes walked out of the room was awkward for me. At first I apologized to these teachers and tried to reason with him, explaining that he should do as he was told. But when Wilf was calm and away from the incidents, he could always clearly tell me why he'd acted like he had, and it always felt reasonable.

I never knew a child could say no at school and I had no map in my mind for what it would look like if they did, but once Wilf realized he couldn't be forced, there was no stopping him.

During this period a teacher told me one parents evening that there were two children in class with learning and attention difficulties and that the other one also didn't do the work, but he sat quietly at his desk and cried almost every day.

Wilf was disruptive in his refusals and often walked. I was made to feel that the boy who sat there broken and crying, not advocating for himself, was easier for the teacher to help. What she meant was he was easier to control and he didn't affect the others so much. I said nothing to Wilf that would encourage his defiance, but I started to feel a sense of quiet respect for my child and a relief that he wasn't defeated.

Deep down he knew this environment wasn't healthy for him, and he knew he didn't have enough support, so he truthfully let the cards fall where the cards were going to fall.

Wilf has taught me over the years to question what is expected and put my own needs at the centre of my decisions, to live with more integrity. I found it very hard to say no or displease others even when I was suffering in consequence. As I've got older, I've realized that I have difficulties with setting and maintaining boundaries. Wilf's been inspirational in that way. He's shown me the importance of saying no and walking away when things aren't healthy for me. When you say no to one wrong thing, however excruciating that is, it opens your life up to other more fulfilling opportunities and eventually all those truthful choices lead you to a precious life.

PAUSE AND REFLECT

What is one good thing that the way in which your child shows up in the world has taught you?

. . . .

. . . .

. . . .

. . . .

. . . .

. . . .

. . . .

. . . .

It may be that their excitement and enthusiasm has made you more grateful for small things. Perhaps their literal interpretation of events or commentary has made you appreciate honest and straightforward communication. The way they think out of the box might have stirred you to be more creative in your approach to life, or their love of animals may have encouraged you to grow your knowledge and relationship with animals. Maybe you got a pet you never thought you needed but now adore. Perhaps one of your child's obsessions has become interesting to you too, and you are now very educated in the Triassic period or have given yourself permission to buy that Lego® set you always wanted because adults like to build and play too when given a chance. Maybe you never knew how to bake bread or fancy cakes, but you've had to learn and now you do.

If your child has physical disabilities and is unable to do many things, how do they cope with that and where do they find pockets of joy or comfort? What has that taught you?

I love this quote by writer and blogger Cassie Hilt: 'They are every good part of your soul and every brave bone that you are missing.' Just read that out loud for a moment and let it sink in. 'They are every good part of your soul. And every brave bone that you are missing.' I don't know if that lands with you but it sure as hell did for me. My children are soulful and brave. They shine brightly, and so do yours I'm pretty sure. All children do at essence.

PART FOUR

When all else fails, know this

70% of parenting is getting it wrong, but every mistake is a golden opportunity to love and reconnect with your child

Getting It Wrong Is Getting It Right

If you've read anything here or in other books that made you sit up straight and think, 'Oh no, I've been getting that wrong, don't panic. Parenting is hard. We have to learn as we go along, because all children are individuals.

And everything you're reading about – I have got wrong before I've got it sometimes right. I'm still getting things wrong all the time. Even in the knowing of the right way to act, I'm still in the learning process with you. Slowly I'm developing more self-awareness.

Sometimes I see what happened after it happened. Sometimes I know what I should do in the moment to help myself, but I still press the easy button or rant and rave because I'm dysregulated and don't have the benefit of perspective. It's not straightforward. But like a person learning to run 5K, I'm gradually getting to the point where weeks, months and years down the line some of the things are taking hold. It's getting more intuitive.

I know that, like me, you are a loving parent with good intentions. How do I know? Because you're reading this and trying your hardest to be the best version of yourself. So, give yourself a break, ok? AND... this is going to make you cry with happiness: parenting expert Dr Becky Kennedy tells us that repair is the single most important part of parenting. Not getting it right, but apologizing and reconnecting after getting it wrong. That's where the gold is.

Apologizing may seem like it's going to make you feel vulnerable. You might fear your child's judgement or think you'll be highlighting something your child may not have noticed. But even when they haven't consciously clocked a wrong, their bodies will have noticed. It will all be in there.

And our brains and our attachment styles (attachment trauma) are rewiring all the time, so if you feel like you got some stuff wrong, share that with them. It helps them to grow and builds trust and connection between you.

Amanda Doyle researched this for the *We Can Do Hard Things* podcast (I know I quote that show a lot – just listen to it!) and discovered studies showing that if you were to be aligned with your child 100% of the time (which by the way is impossible) it would actually do them no good at all, because your child would learn to expect a perfect love later on in life, which is something they'll never be able to replicate.

If you're making mistakes and getting it wrong 70% of the time with your child, but you are coming back and repairing, what they learn is the basis for a healthy, growing relationship. They come to understand that people who love each other are imperfect, that they're going to screw up, and what you should expect of people that love you is that when they get it wrong they're going to come to you and apologize. They are going to own their mistakes and take responsibility for them.

I have found a lot of freedom in this concept. I hold up my hands all the time and find it a relief to do so. It has also gained me a lot more respect from both of my children. We all understand that just like they are good kids doing their best and losing their shit sometimes, I also, despite having the very best intentions to be a good mum, get things wrong a lot and lose *my* shit sometimes. We're all human.

Harriet Lerner (who is also an expert in over- and under-functioning) has written an amazing book called *Why Won't You Apologize? Healing Big Betrayals and Everyday Hurts.* Apologizing is so misunderstood. It's weighted and scary for many people so in case you don't have time to floss your teeth, let alone read a whole book on apologizing, the main points are:

- *I'm sorry* is one of the two most important things to say in a relationship where you love someone. It allows your relationship to grow, so it really matters.

- Don't expect or ask for forgiveness. It turns out that that is not something that can be sought. It happens or doesn't happen over time.

- When an apology is done right, it's very healing. When it isn't done right, it can close the other person down within the relationship.

So how do we go about it? I think first it's helpful to explore why we find apologizing so hard.

It may be that you grew up in a household where it wasn't safe to apologize. Perhaps if you apologized for one thing, you'd be scapegoated for more things. Would you be blamed for everything? Were you and your siblings pushing blame about because your parents got explosive when things got broken or used without permission or you were late? Did your own parents role-model apologizing, or did they get defensive and tell you it didn't happen like you experienced it, you got it wrong and it's not actually their fault?

If you accepted responsibility, perhaps your parent would shout or lecture. They might use your apology to regain control and discipline you, which would make apologizing very off-putting. It's likely that our parents' generation pre the internet and self-help psychology didn't have the information we do today. They were doing their best, in the dark, having been parented quite heavy-handedly themselves in most cases.

So, to sum up, chances are there were unpleasant consequences to apologizing and overwhelming feelings of shame that have left you feeling defensive when criticized.

PAUSE AND REFLECT

Take a moment to consider or write about your experiences with apologies.

What happened if you apologized as a child? It might help to unpack what the reactions were in the moment, how your parents reacted, how your siblings if you had them reacted. What happened afterwards? Did people change how they acted around you and for how long following an apology?

What did you feel?

. . . .

. . . .

. . . .

. . . .

Did your parents or carers ever apologize to you?

. . . .

. . . .

. . . .

. . . .

If so, did you feel heard? Describe the way in which they apologized and how you felt at the end of it. If this all feels a very long time ago, just sit with it for a moment or a few days. Reach in. Your body will still know.

. . . .

. . . .

. . . .

. . . .

SOMETHING PRACTICAL TO TRY...

Things we're scared of when we apologize:

- Having got something wrong – does it make us a bad person?

- Giving the other person the edge – will they now blame us for everything?

- Will they act self-righteously and believe they are better than us if we admit our fault in the matter?

- Will they weaponize our flaws and shoot them back at us to prove points in the future or avoid taking the blame themselves?

- Will they discipline us – lecture us in how we're flawed or falling short?

- Will they be angrier towards us? Feel justified in their anger or disappointment?

- Will it harm our relationship? Will they resent us for getting it wrong?

- Fear of not having your apology accepted.

- Feeling shame/small/vulnerable/out of control.

- Not feeling good enough.

Can you recognize thinking or feeling any of these?
Underline any that stand out for you.

I was on my own journey with apologizing, both as a daughter and a mother, when I stumbled across Harriet Lerner's work. So I'd experienced it from both angles. But Harriet wrote some stuff that was just so incredibly clarifying: that admitting our weaknesses and challenging the image we have of the best version of ourselves are tough. Doing this can make you defensive and that's not relationship building.

Do you ever catch yourself building your defence whilst your child is talking? Looking for all the ways in which what they're saying is exaggerated or not quite true? The inaccuracies, the reasons and justifications around why you did the thing you did or said the thing you said? The one time that what they are saying wasn't true? How they are just not seeing the full picture or what your intention was?

The problem is that whilst we're building our case, we're not listening. We're not discovering what our child is feeling, and that means our relationship with them can't grow. A lack of apology leaves us disconnected, which over time can lead to a wall forming between us.

Strangely enough, when you are in a loving relationship, all those things you fear the apology will unleash don't happen if you get the apology right. There's a sense of empowerment that comes with a good apology. It's a gift to the person receiving it because they feel heard and soothed, but it turns out that it's a gift to yourself too.

In most situations, especially with children who look up to you and love you, you will be more respected. And if the child or young person doesn't respond positively, you still stand on firmer ground. You'll literally feel it in your body, a solid, more secure feeling as you grow in resilience and self-esteem, one apology at a time.

Apologies are truly a gift to your parent–child relationship. Intimacy relies on that repair, the trust that everyone is heard and that we'll work hard to listen to each other with curiosity because we don't want to go about hurting each other and repeating our mistakes. They mean we can bring our hurts to each other in the safety and knowledge that they will be seen, and this in turn allows our relationship to grow. Without it, one or both people are holding back or holding stuff in, and this builds a wall of disconnection. It's worth keeping that front and centre when you're feeling vulnerable and defensive.

Here is Harriet Lerner's advice on how to apologize well (with the parent–child dynamic at the centre):

- No *buts*. Don't say, 'I'm sorry, but this is what I was thinking...' (*buts* are criticism, justifications and excuses).

- Keep the focus on your actions and not the other

person's response. Don't say, 'I'm sorry you felt hurt by this or that.' Just say, 'I'm sorry I did this.'

- A good apology offers a resolution or restoration. How are you taking actions to make it right? What corrective behaviour?

- Don't be dismissive and short in your apologies.

- And don't over-apologize for everything as if you're scared to take up space. If you say, 'I'm sorry I got it wrong. I'm the worst parent ever. I feel awful,' then your children have to caretake your feelings. It's more emotional work for them on top of what happened. It's no longer an apology, it's an invitation for them to take care of you.

- Don't get caught up in who started it or who is more to blame. Apologize for your part, even if your child cannot see or take responsibility for their part. Even if you feel your part is 5% – be the role model.

- A true apology should not set about to silence another person. I'm sorry as a shutdown, so you don't have to listen to them any more, is not useful to your relationship.

- You shouldn't offer an apology to make you feel better, if it makes your child feel worse. It's not there to help soothe you and make you feel less guilty or to explain yourself. If your child is taking space and doesn't want to hear it or see you right then, you must respect that.

- A good apology does not ask the child to do anything, to rush them to be over it, to apologize back for their side of things, not even to forgive you.

- It's also not a bargaining tool – to stop the upset and get back to normal so we can do this or that with the rest of our day.

There's a lot there to unpack. Look through each point and decide whether this is something you typically do. Underline the problem areas that you need to look out for.

To simplify things this is what you are aiming for:

- Listen out for the essence of why your child feels hurt.

- Place the relationship at the centre.

- Be curious as to how you may have got this wrong – curiosity changes everything.

- Apologize for your part (your part is anything you can agree with – even if in your mind it's 5%) without justifications.

- Don't argue back – ask calm questions about anything you don't understand.

- Be wholehearted in your manner and tone of voice.

Appreciate that it will have been hard for your child to bring this to you. When they rock the boat, they may fear losing your love, getting the cold shoulder or you exploding. They have brought it to you as an investment in your relationship. If you are overwhelmed by a long list of complaints, there's no harm in asking for one issue at a time, explaining you're finding it hard to take it all in at once. And if you're triggered and not in the best frame of mind to listen, can you be upfront about this and make a time you'll come back calmer and ready to hear? Harriet says that a new and neutral place to discuss can be very beneficial. In my experience walking side by side in a peaceful environment can be helpful.

If your child apologizes for any part they feel was their responsibility, just thank them. Don't say, 'It's fine, don't worry' – that belittles what has happened as ok. Don't use this moment to teach them more about why what they did was wrong. Just a simple thank-you. Anything you want to say about what happened can keep for another day. If you respond in this way, it will leave more ease and space for apologies in the future.

You may end the apology chat with different opinions. You may not entirely agree with everything your child is saying. But look for the parts you can agree with, make your apology for them. And know that it's ok to discuss which bits you see differently and don't feel responsible for, as long as it isn't coming from a defensive place. Relationships, after all, require being tolerant of all our differences. But check in with your body and tone of voice to make sure. Do you genuinely not agree? Or is this an unconscious protective strategy? It might be hard to discern this at first.

If you discover with hindsight or reflection that your apology was a bit skew-whiff, why not ask your child if you can do it again? Establish a sense of security in the relationship between you by explaining that they are a good kid with a good heart and good intentions and sometimes they get things wrong, and how you are the same, good at heart. How you both love each other and that it's important to be curious about what each other is saying. Perhaps you were a bit defensive before or felt ashamed or triggered. Explain what happened inside you and that you'd like to give it another go with the relationship between you both at the centre of it all. This time listen and feel curious. Instead of looking for inaccuracies and what you don't agree with, look for what could be true.

Could you hold a family meeting where you explain what you've learned about apologizing so that the children can understand how it works? Could you go through some role-playing with your child whilst you both learn how it goes? Start with small, wacky scenarios that aren't too close to home and explore how each person feels hearing the other's words.

For those that find all this hard, that's ok. It is hard to start with. But I promise it comes good with only a small bit of practice. I think the beauty in all of this is that through learning how to apologize and repair we are setting our kids up with great skills for the future. One day they might have a friendship, a partnership or children of their own. They are going to get stuff wrong too. But if they knew how to avoid the brick walls, how to stay connected to those loved ones that they wrong and that sometimes wrong them, then that's a massive gift. And one that makes me sleep better at night.

Useful to know:

- Apologizing is important, but you need to be in a safe, healthy relationship where apologizing is or can become a tool for growing and changing.

- Sometimes it's healthier for the person not to forgive, in situations where forgiveness is giving permission for repeated behaviours, or the behaviour has been so hurtful that it is inappropriate to forgive.

Life Is a Rollercoaster

Isn't it? The truth is that whether you are married or single, have children or pets or live alone, work or stay at home, every single day is up and down. You can think that a day has been bad, but if you really dug into it, you could easily find five to ten things to be grateful for. On any given day.

I know this because even in my darkest hours, crying myself to sleep, I have used my fingers to list ten things, and although some days it takes me longer than others, there's always ten. Even when someone extremely special has died. There's always love and kindness of sorts – a note from a neighbour, a cat on your lap, a hug from a friend, a meal made by your partner, a meal made by you (and other acts of self-love), a cup of coffee in the sunshine – and usually four walls keeping us dry and warm. Listing them at night has made me notice them in the day more. Little, tiny pockets of warmth, joy, fun and connection. Not whole days, pockets. That's the same for everyone, and yet sometimes we focus on them more than others. Sometimes we have our lens so focused on the challenges that the lighter moments are dismissed.

I've also noticed that there are bad days for the kids, that can be followed, totally unexpectedly, by a great day; and great days that lead you into a false sense of security, only to hit you with a bad day. Sometimes everything feels plain sailing for a few weeks as your child matures; and sometimes it's rough seas. The pockets are still there, but it's harder to grasp them. But whatever moment you're in, you can rest assured that in time everything passes, like the weather moving across the sky.

If you find yourself in a storm, hold tight. Breathe out. Find your centre line, what your core needs are, and in that soft landing place know that it'll pass. On a good day, write a three to five point emergency gap plan and stick it on the fridge for easy access, because it's hard to remember what's good for us when we're in our stress responses, just like it's hard for our kids to make 'good choices' when they are in theirs.

These are the times to be kind, be creative and attend to yourself with radical self-care, even when that feels ridiculous or selfish or counter-productive, which it does to start with. Put on the pjs and make soup or the glittery heels and go out dancing.

Everything in this journal has led you down an easier path. That's its aim. Occasionally the questions might have felt hard to answer. There might be new habits that require cultivating, but, honestly, is any of it harder than what you had going before? I hope the sort of hard found in these pages is a sort of growthful hard, rather than the endless hard slog of before.

But whatever the weather in your house, you're not alone. I'm in the thick of it with you. We all are. All those reading this book in the same, tired moment as you, all those that have read it before you and all those still to come:

We love you and we salute you.

Lou, xxx

Note: The thinking throughout this book mostly reflects a moment in time during my journey as a mother. Every time I revisited these pages to edit them, I wanted to change something, add something or take something away as my thoughts and ideas grew, dissolved and evolved again. It's a snapshot. And at first, I was afraid to commit that to publication, a solid book I would need to look in the eye for a lifetime. However, I wrote *Wide Open Spaces* partly to make sense of what had happened to us as a family and partly because at times when I was in the thick of it all I felt so alone. When I could finally take a breath, I sat down and wrote the book I wished could have been my companion, and the only reason for publishing it has been to create a cosy, warm community for all of us.

I'm always onto the next heartfelt and curious thing, so if you'd like to join me in my journey you can find me on my website louisefearn.co.uk, on Instagram @thecuriousparent and listen to my latest meditations on Insight Timer (insight-timer.com/LouFearn). We're going to be ok. xxx

Acknowledgements

I'd like to honour the mentors and teachers who showed me the way. Glennon Doyle, Abby Wambach, Amanda Doyle and Liz Gilbert do not know me, but their voices have saved me from myself countless times. As have the words of Cheryl Strayed, Martha Beck, Jeff Warren and Brené Brown. These soulful beings made me feel less alone in the world and have influenced the way I talk to and love my children, for which they will always have a place in my heart. I don't know where I would be without them, and even though I may never meet them I am hugely grateful that they exist.

And to thank Lynda at Jessica Kingsley Publishers for picking up this manuscript one grey January day and seeing potential in it, who alongside all of the team at JKP brought it to life and sent it out into the world with thought and care.

Thanks also to the family and friends who have been on this journey with me, in particular my own dear mum, Bron, a wise woman who has always lovingly supported me with everything she is and everything she has. I am so utterly blessed to have been mothered by her. To Lucy Gillett for her hugs, hands at my back, weekly walks and wisdom, and Shan Record, Vicki Sagar, Alice Scorer and in particular Rachel Barker, whose love and generosity of spirit have led me on some of the greatest adventures of my life. Also the other incredible women in my women's circle – Shaye, Emma, Amber, Harry, Sarah and Mel – and Lucy Banks and Aino Stennett, who make up my teeny-tiny writer's group: membership of three. I am blessed to know such extraordinary women who have seen me through some tough times. I love you all so much.

And lastly, in memory of my dad, Nick, who always believed in me as both a mother and a writer, even when I didn't believe in myself.

Bibliography

I gratefully acknowledge the following sources.

Part One

Chapter 1 (family gap plan): https://brenebrown.com/podcast/
brene-on-comparative-suffering-the-50-50-myth-and-settling-the-
ball/#transcript

Part Two

Chapter 7 (the 'easy button' and meeting our needs): https://momastery.
com/blog/episode-08

Chapter 9 (play as a source of energy): https://brenebrown.com/podcast/
on-my-mind-rbg-surge-capacity-and-play-as-an-energy-source/#tran-
script

Chapter 10 (Martha Beck): https://momastery.com/blog/we-can-do-hard-
things-ep-67

Chapter 11 ('Big Magic'): *Big Magic* by Elizabeth Gilbert, published by
Bloomsbury, 2016

Chapter 11 (letter to Fear): *Big Magic* by Elizabeth Gilbert, published
by Bloomsbury, 2016, and expanded on in the *Calm Masterclass:
Creative Living Beyond Fear* by Elizabeth Gilbert, www.youtube.com/
watch?v=HHNgqBvhExE

Chapter 12 ('Big Magic'): *Big Magic* by Elizabeth Gilbert, published by
Bloomsbury, 2016

Chapter 12 (permission slip): *Big Magic* by Elizabeth Gilbert, published
by Bloomsbury, 2016, and expanded on in the *Calm Masterclass:
Creative Living Beyond Fear* by Elizabeth Gilbert, www.youtube.com/
watch?v=HHNgqBvhExE

Part Three

Chapter 26 (collaborative solutions): *The Explosive Child: A New Approach for Understanding and Parenting Easily Frustrated, Chronically Inflexible Children* (6th edition) by Dr Ross W. Greene, published by Harper, 2021

Chapter 27 (codependency): Jen Hatmaker talking on the *We Can Do Hard Things* podcast, https://momastery.com/blog/we-can-do-hard-things-ep-86, and on her *For the Love* podcast, https://jenhatmaker.com/podcasts/series-48/going-solo-finding-yourself-and-keeping-hope-alive-jens-thoughts-on-2022

Chapter 28 (Cheryl Strayed): Interviewed on the *We Can Do Hard Things* podcast https://momastery.com/blog/we-can-do-hard-things-ep-197

Part Four

Chapter 30 (reconnecting and apologizing): Amanda Doyle with Dr Becky Kennedy on the *We Can Do Hard Things* podcast, https://momastery.com/blog/we-can-do-hard-things-ep-169

Chapter 30 (apologizing): *Why Won't You Apologise? Healing Big Betrayals and Everyday Hurts* by Harriet Lerner, published by Gallery Books, 2017

Chapter 30 (how to apologize): Harriet Lerner on Brené Brown's *Unlocking Us* podcast, https://brenebrown.com/podcast/harriet-lerner-and-brene-im-sorry-how-to-apologize-why-it-matters-part-1-of-2

YOU THE DADDY

Copyright © Giles Alexander, 2024

Peer reviewed by Lindsay Kerrigan, BSc Midwifery, PgDip Specialist Community Public Health Nursing

An Hachette UK Company
www.hachette.co.uk

Vie Books, an imprint of Summersdale Publishers
Part of Octopus Publishing Group Limited
Carmelite House
50 Victoria Embankment
LONDON
EC4Y 0DZ
UK

www.summersdale.com

Printed and bound in Poland

ISBN: 978-1-83799-125-9

Substantial discounts on bulk quantities of Summersdale books are available to corporations, professional associations and other organizations. For details contact general enquiries: telephone: +44 (0) 1243 771107 or email: enquiries@summersdale.com.